W9-ARR-729

THE
FIELD& STREAM
Sporting
Vehicles
Handbook

The Field & Stream Fishing and Hunting Library

The Field & Stream *Bowhunting Handbook* by Bob Robb
The Field & Stream *Deer Hunting Handbook* by Jerome B. Robinson
The Field & Stream *Firearms Safety Handbook* by Doug Painter
The Field & Stream *Shooting Sports Handbook* by Thomas McIntyre
The Field & Stream *Turkey Hunting Handbook* by Philip Bourjaily
The Field & Stream *Upland Game Handbook* by Bill Tarrant

The Field & Stream *Baits and Rigs Handbook* by C. Boyd Pfeiffer.
The Field & Stream *Bass Fishing Handbook* by Mark Sosin and Bill Dance
The Field & Stream *Fishing Knots Handbook* by Peter Owen
The Field & Stream *Fish Finding Handbook* by Leonard M. Wright Jr.
The Field & Stream *Fly Fishing Handbook* by Leonard M. Wright Jr.
The Field & Stream *Tackle Care and Repair Handbook* by C. Boyd Pfeiffer

THE
FIELD&STREAM
Sporting Vehicles Handbook

Slaton L. White

Photographs by
Peter Mathiesen and Elde Stewart

THE LYONS PRESS

10 9 8 7 6 5 4 3 2 1

Printed in Canada

Library of Congress Cataloging-in-Publication Data

White, Slaton L.
    The Field & Stream sporting vehicles handbook / Slaton L. White
      p.   cm.
    Includes index.
    ISBN 1-58574-092-6 (pbk.)
    1. Sport utility vehicles—Customizing—Handbooks, manuals, etc. 2. Sport utility
vehicles—Off road operation—Handbooks, manuals, etc. I. Field & stream. II. Title.

TL230.5.S66 W49 2000
629.28'732—dc21   00-026293

Contents

Preface		vii
Acknowledgments		ix
Introduction		1
1	Buying a New 4×4	3
2	Buying a Used 4×4	15
3	Fine-Tuning the Suspension	27
4	Picking the Right Tire	38
5	Rolling Along	46
6	When Big Isn't Best	53
7	Locked Tight	61
8	Keeping Transmissions Out of Trouble	68
9	Stop!	77
10	Exhausting Solutions	85
11	Let There Be Light	90
12	Helping Hand	96
13	Matching the Hitch	104
14	Getting Out There . . . and Back	113
15	The Happy Truck Camper	120
16	The Secret to Long Life	128
17	A Tale of Two Trucks	137
18	The Future of High Performance	148
	Appendix	159
	Index	177

Preface

A S DISSIMILAR as their interests may appear at first glance, the outdoorsman and the performance automotive enthusiast are on a technology collision course. Put simply, the utility of contemporary trucks currently being used for hunting, fishing, camping, towing, and other outdoor activities is rapidly being enhanced by the crossover of practices and skills from the performance-car (read "hot rod") community.

Several factors are contributing to this transition. Foremost is the vision of such outdoor proponents as *Field & Stream* Editor Slaton White. Slaton was one of the first to see the wholesale benefits of marrying the truck-owning outdoorsman to the performance product sector.

The other big factor is that truck manufacturers are faced with producing vehicles that are mainstream to the marketplace. As a consequence, new trucks are middle-of-the-road efforts designed to meet a wide variety of buyer personalities, needs, and demands. But, as Slaton has so aptly pointed out for more than a decade in the pages of *Field & Stream,* "outdoorsmen need something more."

That "more" is the crux of this book.

Slaton's crusade—and that's exactly what it is—has been to tell his readers that they don't have to endure the middle-of-the-road performance of a stock pickup or sport utility. At the same time, he has also been a tireless advocate for his reader when he deals with the automotive aftermarket; he constantly reminds industry leaders just how big the outdoor market is and just what kind of performance hunters and fishermen need. When Slaton and I first met a few years ago—while working on a performance truck project—he sat patiently through a long technical explanation of the benefits of upgrading truck exhaust systems. When I finished, he looked up from his notes and said, "Well, what does that mean for my guys?"

"My guys" is *you*—the American Sportsman.

I later found out I was just one in a long chain of industry experts that Slaton has encountered over the years—and each of us has had to consider performance upgrades in terms of functional usefulness for "his guys." It helps us make sure the applications work as intended, and it ensures that the performance products for outdoorsmen have been designed specifically for trucks; they are not relabeled high-performance equipment that has simply been misdirected into the outdoor market.

This *Field & Stream* Handbook is carefully designed to explain the benefits of a wide range of truck upgrades—including the latest on intake and exhaust systems, transmissions, and on-board computers. There are also chapters on such bolt-on accessories as wheels, winches, and lights—all you need to turn the stock pickup into a real hunting and fishing machine. Some of the recommended changes are in the user-friendly and do-it-yourself categories. Others may require the skills of a professional mechanic or installer. In either case, the modifications have been designed to increase the functionality of your pickup.

As Slaton says in the book, "It's a brave new world" of truck performance. But it's a world that is now welcoming the hunter and fisherman.

—JIM MCFARLAND

Acknowledgments

THOUGH A BOOK such as this carries only one name under the title, in many ways it is truly a group effort. I'd like to thank the following individuals for volunteering their expertise as well as their valuable time: Steven Anderson, Flowmaster, Inc.; Charley Cornelius, Can-Back, Inc.; Joel Fischel, Summit Racing Equipment; Mark Heffington, Hypertech, Inc.; Joe Hige, Draw-Tite, Inc.; Jim Jackson and Buddy King, ARB Air Locker, Inc.; Jim McFarland, Autocom, Inc.; Jim Reid, The Coleman Co.; Ron Shivers, DeeZee, Inc.; Laurie Simpson, Alcoa Wheel Products International; Bruce Snyder, Trailmaster Suspension; Gary Steffens, San Bernardino (CA) Sherrif's Department; Steve White, Uniroyal/Michelin North America; and the staff at Superwinch, Inc.

Special thanks go to Jonathan Spiegel and Jeff Cheechov of The Progress Group for taking the time to check—and correct—my "interpretations" of technical material. I also appreciate their sharing some favorite fishing spots with me.

In addition, Brian Appelgate of B&M Racing & Performance Products deserves special mention. Brian has the rare ability to break down complicated technical matters into easy-to-understand language; more important, he was one of the first to understand the depth and breadth of the performance–outdoors marketplace, and his early support helped open many other doors.

Finally, there is the catalyst, the person who helped bring this effort together. Dave Cole is the visionary who first steered me (and *Field & Stream*) into the performance end of the outdoor-automotive arena. In the process he's also become a great fishing partner who understands the power of a river full of trout at last light, a largemouth that takes a spinnerbait on the edge of a tule stand, and a steaming mug of cowboy coffee in a frost-covered mountain camp at first light. He is also author of the phrase, "More Trout, Less Doubt," which has become one of the operating principles in my life.

Introduction

The Price of Adventure

D ARK WAS CLOSING in fast. Mountains gone to purple in the last light cast deep shadows over the trail—a narrow shelf barely wider than the 4×4. Camp was 18 miles in; we still had a long way to go and all I could think was, *Will this truck make it?*

We rounded a turn and I stopped the vehicle to take a look at our dust trail. Dave said, "Don't look down."

"Why?"

"You won't like what you'll see."

"Why?"

"Trust me. It's a long way down."

"Okay. Tell me again why we're doing this?"

"Wild rainbows."

"And the fresh bear scat and the rattlers?"

"The price of adventure, my friend."

I needn't have worried. Our truck, a reconditioned 4×4 compact pickup, proved to be a trailworthy fellow. How it got that way will interest any hunter or fisherman who wants improved performance from his pickup or sport utility. That kind of performance is the subject of this book.

Though the modern pickup is a technological marvel, it is far from perfect, especially if you need it to tow or go offroad. Fortunately, there is a wide variety of products out there designed to enhance the performance of your four-wheel-drive pickup or sport utility. The chapters that follow will explain how upgrades to a truck's suspension system, exhaust system, and electronic engine controls can yield dramatic and much-welcome improvements in towing, load-hauling, and offroad performance. You'll also learn about such critical bolt-on accessories as winches, auxiliary lights, hitches, and wheels. And since this book is designed to get you "out there," I've included offroad driving tips to help you and your vehicle perform better while in the field.

But that's not all. To improve the ultimate usefulness of this book, you'll find several case studies of project vehicles, each of which will help you personalize your truck. To that end, see the appendix for a list of aftermarket manufacturers with addresses, telephone numbers, and website URLs.

Although I've included a chapter with tips on how to buy a new sport utility or pickup, you'll note a distinct focus in this book on used, rather than new, trucks. That's because most folks who spend $30,000 or more for a new four-wheel-drive are terrified to actually take it offroad where briers, buckbrush, prickly pear, or mud, for that matter, might mar the finish of their elegant steed.

In reality, the best vehicles for hunters and fishermen are those, as a dear, departed friend once said, "that wear their mud well." And that usually means older vehicles that can display a scratch as a badge of honor.

Call the concept "The Mobile Sportsman," for such performance allows you to get to those wild places that stir the heart and feed the soul, the places where a deer can magically appear and disappear like a puff of smoke, where a big rainbow trout will rise through broken water to a high-riding dry fly.

We made camp long after last light. Dave's son, Jeremy, had left a lantern on—after the last crest we homed in on it as if it were the Pole Star. For dinner, Jeremy served his Twin Cheese Surprise: a melted mass of cheese on a soft flour tortilla, followed by kielbasa and fried onions, all dished out on a Frisbee. When I asked why, he said, "This area is full of fresh bear scat. I don't want any food on the ground."

I decided to sleep in the truck. *No problemo,* as Jeremy would have phrased it. With extra gear up on the rack and the cap's sliding windows open, I slept through a lightning storm that drifted over the mountain in the middle of the night. And I didn't have one nightmare about bears.

After fishing in the morning, we broke camp and headed home. It was going to be a long ride out, and the temperature was already well on its way to 100° F. But that's the price of adventure. Let's get started.

Buying a New 4×4

You can't always get what you want; but you can get what you need.

O N MY LAST HUNTING TRIP in the South, I stopped at one of those roadside eateries that cater to folks like me who can't resist hand-lettered "BBQ" signs. Once inside the screen door, I stared a long time at the menu, which was nothing more than a painted board nailed above the counter. Finally, the counterman took pity on me.

"It's simple," he said. "Beef."

I nodded.

"'Course, you can take that chopped, sliced, or shredded, with or without sauce, and you got beans and relish on the side. And, we got two sizes—large and extra large."

As I recall, I went whole hog and ordered a huge sandwich with all the trimmings.

Buying a new 4×4 can be similarly gut-wrenching. You start simple, but suddenly you're looking at a vehicle with all the trimmings. The only problem is that a new 4×4 is considerably more expensive than a barbecue sandwich. Careful preparation, however, can keep the heartburn to a minimum.

STARTING OUT

The first step is to determine the type of 4×4 you require. Given the size of the market (more than 50 models), this may seem a Herculean task, but the field breaks down in a hurry into four basic types:

Although there are more than 50 different types of sport utilities and pickups now on the market, the field breaks down into four basic components: full-size sport utilities and pickups, and compact sport utilities and pickups.

full-size and compact sport utilities, and full-size and compact pickup trucks. By and large, full-size vehicles from the same manufacturer share mechanical underpinnings and designs. The same holds true for the compact segment. And broadly speaking, sport utilities will cost more than a comparably equipped pickup.

What type would work best for you? That depends on the kinds of hunting and fishing you do, whether you need the vehicle for work, and if you need to haul your family around as well. Inevitably, you'll have to compromise. Though most sportsmen would like a vehicle dedicated exclusively to hunting and fishing, the majority need their vehicle to do double duty.

Think this through; sometimes the best choice isn't obvious. For example, a Virginia angler I know was looking at compact sport utilities, but then decided on a compact pickup with a cap. Since he didn't have any children and generally fished with one partner, he didn't need to pay for the extra seats of a sport utility.

A full-size sport utility was the only alternative for a Texas sports-

Compact pickups, such as the Ford Ranger, are a good choice for outdoorsmen who prefer a smaller package and who rate fuel economy over brute strength.

Full-size sport utilities, such as the GMC Yukon (twin to the Chevrolet Tahoe), remain a top choice because the vehicles can carry people as well as plenty of gear.

Compact sport utilities, such as the Ford Explorer, really took off in the late 1980s when they came equipped with four doors.

man I know, however, because, as he put it, "I'm a gear hog, and during the fall when I'm after birds, deer, and bass I practically live out of my truck. I need a lot of storage space for me and my partner, and since I drive anywhere from 4 to 6 hours to hunt, I also wanted a cab with some room to stretch out. And when I'm not in the field, the rear seat stays up so I can haul around my family."

A Montana bird hunter recommends a compact sport utility. "There's plenty of room for my pointer, my partners, and all our gear," he says. "In addition, I prefer the fuel economy of the V6 engine to that of a big V8."

Finally, there's the big-game hunter from New Mexico who prefers full-size pickups. "With a big V8 engine, I can tow a big trailer, and with a cap in place I can store enough gear for a week in deer camp. When I'm not hunting, the truck holds all my tools and work supplies."

To each his own. Just remember, what works for a friend may or

Full-size pickups, such as the Dodge Ram, have long been prized by outdoorsmen for their versatility, load-carrying, and towing capability.

may not work for you. And since a new 4×4 will set you back any-where from $20,000 to well over $40,000, don't be in too big a hurry to make up your mind.

THE RIGHT STUFF

After you've established the type of 4×4 you need, it's time to figure out how the vehicle should be equipped. Here's where you really go to work, for nearly every 4×4 on the market offers a mind-boggling array of standard and optional equipment. A partial list includes engine, transmission, four-wheel-drive system, seats, tires, instrument panel, air-conditioning, power doors, windows, and mirrors, fog lamps, and specialty packages (trailer towing, handling, offroad, heavy-duty suspension, and auxiliary cooling).

This equipment may be available by special-option groups or by trim levels. Some of it can be ordered separately. It all depends on the manufacturer.

As you mull all this over, be aware of some important industry trends.

Most new trucks are considerably plusher than before, and inte-rior controls and appointments as well as such basics as ride and han-dling are much more carlike. Utilitarian versions, however, remain in many lines. Just don't expect a dealer to rush you into buying one. (He makes more on upscale versions.) A turkey hunter I know wel-

Most new trucks are considerably plusher than before, and interior controls and appointments as well as such basics as ride and handling are much more carlike.

comed the improved mechanical components but balked at the fancy interiors. He needed an interior that he could hose out after every outing, so he bought a pickup with vinyl bench seats and floor mats, though he had to fight the dealer every step of the way.

Like many hunters and fishermen, you probably think V8s when truck engines come to mind. Nothing wrong with that, especially if you need to haul huge loads. But there are a number of good six-cylinder in-line and V6 engines out there, some of which rival the power of a V8 and offer better fuel economy. You should also think torque rather than horsepower. An engine's torque rating is a truer indication of its ability to work for you. Ideally, you'd like an engine to develop peak torque at a relatively low engine speed—say around

One of the hot trends in full-size pickups these days is extended-cab models that feature four doors.

2,800 to 3,500 revolutions per minute (rpm). (This is especially important if you launch boats off steep ramps or drive on tough offroad trails.)

The federal government is tightening emissions standards as well as raising fuel economy standards for light trucks. As a result, we're beginning to see a profound change in the type of engines found in trucks. The industry standard has been the tried-and-true pushrod design, but Ford and Jeep recently introduced overhead-camshaft engines into some of their products. The difference? The pushrod engine develops high torque at very low rpm, which is perfect for many truck applications. Overhead-camshaft engines typically develop top-end torque at higher rpm, but this engine pollutes less and is more fuel efficient.

The engine's torque is harnessed by the transmission. In the past, many hardcore four-wheelers opted for manual transmissions because of the extra gearing they provided. (Most manuals offer five forward speeds with overdrive for improved fuel economy.) These guys were dissatisfied with automatics that offered only three or four forward speeds; the three speeds had limited gearing, and many four-speeds were plagued by "gear-hunting" computer controls that favored fuel economy over performance.

Most of these problems have been rectified through the introduction of four-speed electronic automatic overdrive transmissions. Still, you'll find that the transmission on a new truck has been designed for ride quality rather than performance. Although new transmissions don't "gear-hunt" as badly as they did a few years ago, you may be less than enthralled with their performance in high-country and towing situations.

A generation ago, four-wheel-drive systems featured manual locking hubs and a manual-shift transfer case. In order to get into and out

A sign of the times. New 4×4s with manual locking hubs are a rarity. Many 4×4s now come with automatic locking hubs and electric-operated transfer cases.

Optional equipment is often grouped in special packages. In some cases (towing, for example), you may need to order more than one package to get all the required equipment.

of 4WD, you had to get out of the cab, lock (or unlock) the hubs on the front wheels, and then shift into (or out) of 4WD. Nowadays, many four-wheel-drive sport utilities and pickups come from the factory with automatic locking hubs and electric-shift transfer cases. You never leave the comfort of the cab to engage 4WD.

Many outdoorsmen don't like the new systems, but they're here to stay. Some models still offer manual-shift transfer cases, though you may have to special-order the vehicle to get them.

As for those special packages, carefully evaluate each one, especially if you plan to tow a trailer or boat. In some cases, you may have to order more than one optional package to get all the required equipment. For example, to get underbody skid plates and heavy-duty shocks, you may be required to order an offroad package and a handling package. Those who tow may need to order a handling package for the shocks and sway bars, a cooling package for heavy-duty radiators and engine and transmission oil, and a trailer-towing package for the wiring harness and the hitch.

Some factory towing packages don't include the hitch; it may be a dealer option. In this case, you can take the truck to a hitch dealer or have the dealer install it. (Many opt for the latter because the cost of the hitch installation can be rolled into the monthly payment.)

Selecting certain options may preclude you from others. For instance, some trailer-towing packages specify automatic transmissions only. And particular engine and rear-axle combinations may not be available because of federal regulations or market availability.

You also need to consider whether the accessories on your current truck—slide-in camper, cap, roof rack, winch, and the like—will fit the new truck. Case in point: New, more aerodynamic trucks use internal rather than external drip rails. If the roof rack on your old truck was designed to fit an external drip rail and you buy a new truck with internal drip rails, you'll need to buy a new rack as well.

SOURCING THE ACCESSORIES

Truck manufacturers have noticed how hot the truck accessory market is these days, and they are rushing into the game by offering some accessories that traditionally have been left exclusively to the after-market. The problem is that truck manufacturers design a product to appeal to a broad, general market. Hunters or fishermen may find that manufacturer-offered accessories don't meet their specific needs.

Much of the rest of this book is devoted to accessories that have been specially designed to meet the needs of hunters and fishermen. Make a point of reading the relevant chapters before you buy any new accessories.

DEALING WITH A DEALER

I don't know anyone who enjoys haggling with a dealer, and the inevitable tug-of-war between buyer and seller makes buying a 4×4 about as pleasant as having your guns scraped. But if you go armed with a firm strategy based on careful research, you can make the experience bearable.

A friend of mine likes to launch a preemptive strike when he enters a dealership. "When I walk in, I'm ready to buy," he told me. "I know exactly what I want down to the last detail. I tell the dealer, 'You're not going to have the truck I need on the lot. I'm going to order it, and you're going to turn a profit for very little work.'"

This approach works when buying a domestic truck. Import truck buyers have much less leeway because you can't special-order from the factory.

A Montana trout fisherman confronts dealers this way: "First, I get the invoice price of the truck. These figures are usually available from libraries, banks, credit unions, or the Internet. Then I call a dealer (I never walk on the floor if I can help it), ask for the sales manager, and tell him I'll buy the truck for "invoice plus $350, straight cash [outside financing]. If the sales manager won't go for it, I may have to offer invoice plus $500, but that's as far as I go. That's plenty of profit for a dealer, because he usually also gets incentive money from the factory. The whole process takes about 2 minutes 30 seconds, and there's no skating around."

The only way to make this system work for you is to do all your homework, know exactly what you want, and be persistent. Also, the "plus" figure will vary. It might be as low as $200 if the vehicle in question isn't selling well, or much more if it's in great demand. If the dealer has plenty of trucks on the lot, he's usually more willing to bargain, but if he has control of his inventory, he'll tell you to take a hike. You also need to make sure the invoice figures are current (last year's won't do) and cover all the options and special equipment you need.

Don't use the process to lowball the dealer with a completely ridiculous offer. Doing so brands you an idiot. Remember, this guy sells trucks 6 days a week, 8 (or more) hours a day. You buy once every ten years. He is not going to sell you a truck at a loss. A fair offer tells him you are serious, and you are more likely to get the truck you want at a price you can bear.

If you live in an area with few dealers, or if you want a red-hot vehicle, you won't be able to bargain as effectively. Even so, have the numbers at your fingertips. Walking into a showroom completely unprepared is a recipe for disaster.

If you can't come to terms that you can live with, walk. Let the salesman know you're willing to buy a different model from another dealer. That will often bring him back to the table with a more reasonable offer. (I must admit that sometimes this doesn't work. I once had a salesman just turn away from me as I walked out the door. I later bought at a better dealership with a terrific service department, so in the end I made the right move.)

Once you strike a deal, don't compare it to the deals engineered by the guys at work or at the gun club. Are you happy with the deal? That's all that matters. Salesmen can cut a deal in many different ways, and unless you're party to every aspect of the negotiations, you can't really judge the merits of a particular sale.

How much truck can you afford? The general rule of thumb is the purchase price should not exceed half of your annual income. And though you need to be cost-conscious, don't underbuy. In order for the truck to perform on target, you must order the needed special equipment. This is no place to scrimp, especially if your hunting and fishing takes you far from the beaten track.

How much truck can you afford? The general rule of thumb is the purchase price should not exceed half of your annual income. This new two-door Explorer Sport, which falls in the compact sport utility class, will run you more than $25,000; a base-level compact pickup may run you nearly $10,000 less.

THE RULE OF THREE

When buying a new 4×4, keep in mind that you're actually engaging in three distinct transactions: buying a new truck, financing it, and unloading the old truck. For best results, keep each transaction separate. Negotiate the price of the new vehicle first. That done, proceed to financing. (Big tip: Call your bank or credit union for their rates before you walk into the showroom. Armed with this information, you may be able to get dealer financing at a lower interest rate.) Finally, you can consider trading in your old truck, though you'll usually do better if you sell it yourself.

A common ploy among salesmen is to mix these transactions. It's a form of voodoo economics in which they take the trade-in, apply it to the down payment, and then offer a longer-term loan—all of which gives the appearance of lowering the purchase price of the new truck. Doing so makes you a three-time loser: You get less for the trade-in, pay more in interest on the loan, and spend more on the truck. The tactic works because most people look only at the monthly loan payment—the lower, the better.

Also be aware that the dealer cost (what the dealer paid for the truck), the manufacturer's suggested list price, and the sticker price (which includes all special equipment, preparation charges, and other fees) are different. So when you talk "price" make sure you and the dealer are speaking the same language.

Is Leasing for You?

Leasing, rather than buying, is a hot trend. In fact, nearly 40 percent of light trucks are leased these days. But is it really for you?

That depends. The big problem for hunters and fishermen is that at the end of the lease (typically 24 months), the lessee (that's you) must pay for any "excess wear and tear" when the vehicle is returned. Given where we drive our trucks when we hunt and fish, you may find that your truck has a number of scratches or small dents. You will pay handsomely for this. You also may not be able to personalize the vehicle. If you want to add a roof rack, brush guard, auxiliary lights, an electric winch, and other bolt-on accessories, you need to find out whether the lessor (the finance company that owns the vehicle) will allow you to make modifications.

In some ways, leasing is a more complicated procedure than buying. There are many financial pitfalls, so you better do your homework before you sign on the dotted line. But a quick way to figure out if leasing may work for you is to answer the following questions:

Leasing may work for you if:
1. You prefer to drive a new, rather than old, truck;
2. You don't mind making monthly payments;
3. You put less than 12,000 miles a year on your truck;
4. You don't expose your truck to "excess wear and tear."

Leasing probably won't work for you if:
1. You prefer to pay off the loan in full and then drive the vehicle for several years thereafter;
2. You drive more than 12,000 miles per year;
3. You routinely drive into areas where brush, rocks, and other hazards can damage the vehicle.

Final Steps

Now that you know exactly what you want, you're ready to deal. Just remember that knowledgeable truck salesmen are a rare breed, which is why you need to do so much work beforehand. The complex option order codes don't help matters, either. Last year, as a hunting buddy wrestled over an order form at a local dealership, the exasperated salesman told him, "I wish you were ordering a car. It's so much easier."

After the order was completed, my friend double-checked the paperwork to make sure all the information was entered correctly. When the truck arrived, he checked the order against the invoice to make sure everything was in place. Smart move. Do the same. Truck buying is definitely an area where *caveat emptor* reigns supreme.

Finally, since some truck owners purchase new vehicles only every ten years or so, sticker shock is a big problem. The truck that cost you $15,000 ten years ago will probably run more than $25,000 today. If that seems beyond your means, you can take another tack by buying a used 4×4, a subject we'll discuss in the next chapter.

Buying a Used 4×4

How to avoid someone else's trouble.

O NE OF MY FATHER'S ironclad rules of life was, "Never buy someone else's trouble." Of course, the first time I heard that pronouncement was right after I came home with my first used car, purchased "as is" from a lot near the construction site where I had sweated out a summer in purgatory carrying armored cable and ³/₄-inch electrical pipe.

He told me I had squandered my money. I defended myself vehemently, which triggered another of his aphorisms: "Never argue with an idiot." I stomped off in righteous indignation, but came to my senses when the transmission failed shortly thereafter. I was out $400—a month's pay. At least I didn't make the same mistake twice.

RISKY BUSINESS

Buying any used vehicle is risky business. Hunters and fishermen interested in four-wheel-drive versions face additional worries, mainly because of the extra driveline components and the wear and tear of hard offroad use.

Still, buying a used pickup or sport utility remains an appealing proposition, mainly because of the attractive purchase price. New 4×4s can easily run to well over $30,000; however, they depreciate quickly, losing (on average) half of their value within three years. By targeting a 4×4 that's three to five years old, you stand to pick up a solid performer at a substantial savings. Also, used vehicles, by and large, are cheaper to insure.

The best buys are sport utilities and pickups that are three to five years old. But rising prices for new 4×4s have pulled up prices for used 4×4s, which may force you to buy an older vehicle. The now out-of-production Ford Bronco remains a popular choice for many hunters and fishermen.

THE SEARCH

Let's say you're in the market for a used 4×4. Where do you begin? First, develop a profile of the truck you want. This is necessary because trucks come in many models and load designations. For instance, if you're looking at a full-size pickup, you may face as many as a half-dozen engine combinations, the choice of a manual or automatic transmission, three payload ratings ($1/2$-, $3/4$-, and 1-ton) regular or extended cab, plus option packages such as heavy-duty suspension, towing, offroad handling, and heavy-duty cooling. The vehicle profile helps keep the confusion manageable.

The profile should also take into consideration the intended use of the truck. For example, are you primarily interested in towing? Or

Another stalwart for outdoorsmen is the old (full-size) Chevy Blazer. Though it only featured two doors, the back held a hogshead of gear.

What type of used 4×4 is best for you? That depends on many different factors, including whether you drive on difficult offroad trails, tow a bass boat or heavy trailer, or need the vehicle to do double-duty as a family hauler. Think carefully before you buy. Though many prospective buyers immediately think sport utility, sometimes a pickup is a more versatile, and therefore more appropriate, choice.

would you rather buy a shorter wheelbase version for heavy-duty offroad use? Do you want plush interior amenities, or do you prefer the truck to have an interior that can be hosed out after an outing in the mud?

The profile can help you intelligently evaluate each prospect and quickly eliminate those that lack the required features. Your individual budget will no doubt be a big factor in determining exactly what kind of truck you end up owning, so you should also develop a list of acceptable tradeoffs that will help you keep within your price range.

The process is a lot like buying a new vehicle: You still want to make sure the intended vehicle is equipped to do the job. The big difference here is that you'll need to thoroughly look over used 4×4s, keeping a sharp eye for signs of abusive wear and tear. Be sure you aren't buying someone else's trouble.

By "wear and tear" I don't mean ordinary dents and scratches. In the 4×4 world, such blemishes can be expected. In fact, some sellers count on being able to pawn off a truck with major mechanical problems by sprucing up the exterior and cleaning up the interior. On the other hand, a truck in perfect working order may have a weathered appearance that could put you off if you don't look beyond the surface.

Follow the lead of a Texas quail hunter who acquired a three-year-old sport utility that had some warts—minor cosmetic problems—

Always view a used 4×4 during the day. At night, you can easily miss signs of corrosion or leaks. If possible, have a friend accompany you. Two pairs of eyes are better than one.
E. Stewart

but was in great mechanical condition. Describing his purchase, he said, "This dog can hunt!"

Wear and tear can be a sign that some deeper problems exist, however. Look for signs that indicate corrosion, collisions, leaks, and excessive wear. Always view a used 4×4 during the day, as you can easily miss these warnings at night. Avoid rainy days as well; you won't be able to see any leaks. If possible, have a friend accompany you. Two pairs of eyes are better than one, and some inspection routines need two people. Listed below are some of the things to look for. (See the Appendix for an evaluation chart that you can bring with you.)

STEP BY STEP

Examine the outside appearance. Start at one corner and walk around the vehicle, checking the lower areas (the areas most susceptible to corrosion damage) first. Then move to the upper-body panels and make another circuit. Does the paint match all around? Color variations, as well as poorly fitting doors, body panels, or hood may mean the vehicle was in an accident. A fresh coat of paint is also suspect. What's it hiding?

Look underneath for puddles, which can mean leaks from the cooling system, transmission, brakes, or engine. Get under the vehicle and check the frame for cracks or other signs of fatigue. Note damage to skid plates, steering linkages, cables, hoses, wire harnesses, and so on. Inspect the suspension (springs, shock absorbers, and bushings), driveline components (shafts and U-joints), and exhaust system for signs of wear and tear.

Is the underside caked with mud and grime? If it is, you'll most likely inherit a corrosion problem. If the pickup has a bedliner, check

Push down on each corner of the vehicle. If it bounces more than once before leveling off, chances are the shock absorbers need to be replaced.
E. Stewart

Climb inside. The windows should move freely and the seats should be free of rips and tears. If the inside reeks of a heavy masking scent, suspect a wet interior.
E. Stewart

the surrounding sheet metal for signs of corrosion. Look carefully along the underside of the cargo bed for rust.

How are the tires? Uneven tire wear probably means improper wheel alignment, but it can also be a sign of accident damage. Find out. Don't forget the spare, and make sure the jack and other tire-changing equipment are in place and in good working order.

Push down on each corner of the vehicle. If it bounces more than once before leveling off, it probably needs new shock absorbers. Stand about 10 feet in front of the truck. Is it listing to one side? If one side of the truck hangs lower than the other, it may need new springs.

Climb inside. If you detect a musty or moldy odor, suspect a wet interior. (If the interior reeks of a heavy masking scent, suspect the same.) Seats should be free of rips and tears and should not sag when you sit down. All windows should move freely up and down, and all doors should open, close, and lock properly (don't forget the tail-gate). With your helper outside, turn on the lights (low and high beam), turn signals, back-up lights, and so on.

Don't forget to inspect accessory equipment such as caps, roof racks, winches, and brush guards. Check each thoroughly.

ENGINE

The engine is a big-ticket item. Take the time to evaluate it carefully. Open the hood and look around. Is the engine compartment reasonably clean? A filthy mess of oil and baked-on crud may indicate a lack of routine maintenance. Inspect all hoses and belts. If the engine is warm when you arrive, the seller may be trying to hide cold-start problems.

Look at the tailpipe. Black smoke means a problem with the fuel system, which may be corrected by a simple adjustment. Blue smoke means burning oil, and white smoke (at any other time than start-up on a cold morning) means coolant is seeping into the cylinders.

Here's a simple test: Run your finger around the inside of the tailpipe. Signs of oil moisture point to a "burner." A soft sooty substance suggests periodic cylinder misfire, a retarded spark ignition system, or an overly rich mixture condition. Any or all of these warrant a further check to determine the nature and extent of the problem. For example, a partially clogged air cleaner element (cheap fix) can leave the same signs as an overly rich fuel mixture (expensive fix). If the material that rubs off on your finger is dry, the engine passes this first step.

Beyond the tailpipe test, three basic telltale areas help you determine the overall health of the engine: cylinder pressure, coolant, and spark plugs.

Cylinder pressure reveals the operating condition of valves, piston rings, valve seals, and cylinder head gaskets, as well as cracks in the head and block. Experienced shadetree mechanics probably have the equipment required for such tests. If you don't have the tools or the experience, don't worry. These tests can be performed by a professional mechanic for you.

Run your finger around the inside of the tailpipe. If your finger picks up a moist, sooty substance, the engine may be burning too much oil, a problem you don't need to inherit. If the soot is dry, the engine is running fine.
E. Stewart

Remove the radiator cap while the engine is cold. Then start the engine and let it warm up. If bubbles appear in the coolant, the vehicle may have a problem with the head gasket.
E. Stewart

Coolant is another important indicator of overall engine health. Remove the radiator cap while the engine is cold. Start the engine and let it warm up by operating it at moderate (2,000 to 2,500) rpm. If bubbles appear in the coolant, as viewed through the radiator fill spout, you may have head gasket or head/block cracks. If possible, drain a small amount of coolant from the radiator until the upper portion of the core is exposed. Look at the condition of the core. It should be clean and rust-free. Gum, sludge, rust, or a combination of all three indicate a lack of proper maintenance.

Spark plugs are, in many ways, the barometer of an engine's condition. This inspection can be performed by you or by a pro. You're looking for dry, clean porcelain and a deposit-free appearance. A tan to light brown coloring on the porcelain insulator and electrode is a good sign of a well-tuned engine. A sooty coating on any part of the plug (center wire, ground strap, or body) often indicates an overly rich air/fuel mixture. A shiny or oily appearance on these parts suggests excessive oil in the combustion chamber. Plugs with a heat range higher than that recommended by the truck manufacturer often indicate that the owner has tried to prevent plug fouling. This situation requires further investigation.

Small deposits of metal (aluminum, typically) on the porcelain normally mean the engine has been running in detonation (commonly known as knock). This is not good. Knock is a certified engine killer. Move on to another vehicle.

If all plugs appear to be colored acceptably, but one or two fail the test, suspect malfunctioning spark plug wires before you fault the cylinder in question. In fact, comparing the questionable plug readings with the cylinder pressure check will either verify or eliminate bad wires.

TEST DRIVE

If the truck passes muster so far, begin the test drive. The truck should start quickly even when cold, and the transmission should engage smoothly, without loud clanks. The clutch on a manual transmission needs to be checked. If it engages late (pedal almost all the way up) or doesn't have about 1 inch of free play at the top, it probably needs to be replaced. Find an inclined driveway and try backing up the slope. If the clutch chatters or slips under these conditions, it needs to be replaced. With an automatic, hold one foot on the brake while shifting into drive and reverse. Delays in engagement indicate problems you want to avoid. Have a companion stand behind the truck as you drive slowly away. The vehicle should track straight. If the front and rear wheels are not exactly in line, the vehicle is side-tracking (an indication of serious body, frame, or alignment problems).

On the road, the truck should accelerate smoothly without hesitation or unusual noise and should not lose power on hills. Roll down the window and listen for excessive noise from the exhaust system. Let off the throttle and listen for rear-end noises, and brake often to see if the truck veers to one side. A spongy brake pedal could mean problems with the brake lines. The steering should be smooth and vibration-free, with little free play in the wheel.

On a bumpy section of road, see if the vehicle bottoms out or hops to one side—signs of suspension problems. Listen for squeaks and rattles too.

Shift into high-range and low-range 4WD. Make sure it engages and disengages easily and smoothly. Listen for any loud or unusual noises.

Check the vehicle thoroughly for signs of excess wear and tear and missing or damaged equipment. Here, the 4x4 is missing the passenger side mirror.
E. Stewart

After driving, let the engine idle for 10 minutes. Check for signs of rough idle or overheating. Pull out the automatic transmission fluid dipstick and smell it. If the fluid gives off a burnt odor, serious trouble awaits. Shut off the engine and check the engine oil. It should be clean. Let the truck sit for 5 minutes, then restart it. The engine should kick over immediately.

HOME STRETCH

If the truck makes it this far, arrange to have a professional 4×4 mechanic (one whom you trust) put the truck on a lift and go over it again. (If the owner hesitates or balks at your request, take it as a sign that something, somewhere, is "real bad wrong" with the truck. Go elsewhere.) Make sure the mechanic checks the front and rear differentials, wheel bearings, U-joints, and axles for signs of damage. Have him prepare a written estimate for any repairs. That way, you'll have some leverage when haggling.

Assuming the truck clears this hurdle, you're ready to make an offer. Prices vary by region and season. You'll probably pay more if you live near a big city, less in a rural area. The old rule was that prices rise in the summer and drop in the winter. Given the current

The last step is haggling with the owner. Given the popularity of 4×4s these days, used vehicles will cost more than before. Do research so you know the average price of the 4×4 you're interested in. That way you can bargain more effectively.
E. Stewart

popularity of 4WD trucks in suburban areas, you very well may see prices rise in the fall as bad weather sets in. Some models also hold their value much better than others. The *Kelley Blue Book* (www.kbb.com) can help give you an idea of what the average retail price for the vehicle you're interested in is.

The preceding mainly applies to vehicles that are three to five years old. If your budget requires you to shop for vehicles older than that, you can still follow the basic outline, but obviously you will see many more signs of wear and tear. (Some sportsmen may be looking at vehicles as old as ten years. If that's the case, read on.)

Plain and simple, the whole process—particularly the persistent attention to detail—can wear you out. Here, it helps to be able to summon the exasperating wariness of a big brown trout. Do that and you won't buy someone else's trouble.

THE OTHER ROAD

Like many young men, Jeremy Cole is no stranger to empty pockets. But this 25-year-old California outdoorsman hasn't let his personal budget shortfalls keep him from pursuing his outdoor passions. Lately, this passion has fueled the desire to own his first 4×4. "The idea," he said, "is to use the truck to get a little farther in. Then I can hike to spots beyond the reach of most fishermen."

Cole realized that a new 4×4 was out of the question. But he was surprised to learn just how expensive the best of the used 4×4s (vehicles three to five years old) have become. "I couldn't believe the prices I saw when I visited a local dealer," he said. "There wasn't anything that I could afford."

Cole's sticker shock is fallout from the unprecedented popularity of four-wheel-drive vehicles these days. As the prices for new 4×4s skyrocket in response to the demand, the prices for used models are also pulled upward. Unfortunately, this trend leaves outdoorsmen on tight budgets out in the cold.

But Cole was resolute, and his resolve started him down a different road. Once he decided to abandon the safety net (such as it is) of a dealership—which usually offers a limited warranty on what it sells—he realized that his truck was probably within reach. It's a risky road that often requires an investment in sweat equity, but it can lead to a big payoff—as long as you proceed cautiously.

"I started looking through one of those 'auto shoppers' that I found at the 7-11," he said. "The first thing I realized was that I would have to settle for a vehicle far older than what I wanted originally."

In Cole's case, his budget commanded him to look at high-mileage models. When he got to ten-year-old trucks, he started to see prices he could afford.

Cole then checked out government, business, and commercial auctions. (If you go this route, be forewarned: You can get a great deal, but you can also end up with a useless heap. It's strictly *caveat emptor*.) Then he browsed the Yellow Pages. Under "Trucks and Equipment," he struck pay dirt when he found a local dealer who specialized in brokering used equipment for large companies and public utilities.

Cole stopped by and saw a truck with promise: a 1986 GMC S-15 4×4 pickup with just under 100,000 miles. "It had the 2.8-liter V6 and an automatic transmission," he said. "When I first saw it, it had a pretty ugly ding on the rear panel, rust in the bed, and the shadow of 'So Cal Edison' was still visible where the utility's logo used to be. The interior was worn but undamaged. Overall, it seemed in decent mechanical shape, but it really needed a facelift. The paint had turned to chalk in the hot California sun."

The price was right—$5,000, as is. But before he plunked down his cash, Cole had an expert look over the vehicle for serious mechanical defects.

After the truck passed inspection, Cole began the job of turning the truck into a hunting/fishing machine. His first job: an affordable body and paint restoration (see the Appendix).

WHERE TO BUY

- New Car Dealerships: Prices are usually above book value, but good trade-ins can often be found (they get rid of the heaps). Warranties available.
- Used Car Lots: Some good buys can be had, but many of the worst—wrecks, rusted hulks, recovered thefts, and repossessions—end up here. Use caution. The advantage is that you may be able to buy close to the vehicle's wholesale price.
- Dealer Auctions: If you know someone with a dealer's license, attend an auction with him, and pay him a couple of hundred

dollars to act as a middleman. Vehicles are sold at below whole-sale prices, come with some guarantee, and are required to have notice of hidden problems.

- Government Auctions: Dirt-cheap, low-option, and usually well worn. Forget military surplus.

- People You Know: This can be the best source because you should be able to get a complete history of the vehicle. The downside is that problems which develop later may strain a friendship. Since you won't get a warranty, perform a thorough inspection before you buy.

- People You Don't Know: You'll have almost no practical legal recourse if something goes wrong later, so proceed with caution. Good buys can be found, however, which justifies the risk. Most likely you'll phone the owner in response to an ad. Many vehicles are grossly misrepresented, so ask specific questions. For example, "Is there any rust showing?" is better than, "Is it in good condition?" Ask to see the service invoices. The more frequently the oil and filter have been changed, the better.

Fine-Tuning
the Suspension

Rock 'n' roll.

PART 1: TROUBLESHOOTING THE SUSPENSION

OUT OF SIGHT, out of mind. That pretty much sums up how most outdoorsmen view the suspension on their 4×4—until the truck starts bottoming out on rutted trails or groaning like some ghoul in a third-rate direct-to-video horror movie. By this point, you've no doubt figured out that something is dreadfully wrong with the vehicle's ride or handling, but you can't exactly nail down the problem. What do you do?

LOOK AND LISTEN

You can help a suspension expert if you conduct a "look and listen" inspection of your rig before taking it to the shop. You'll need a buddy to help you, preferably one who has not spent a lot of time in the vehicle. (This way he'll be tuned in to problems that have appeared so gradually you no longer notice them.)

According to the folks at Trailmaster Suspension, your inspection should be as follows:

1. Put your buddy behind the wheel while you slip under the front end. Have him turn the key to unlock the steering column (don't start the engine) and slightly wiggle the wheel back and forth. Is there excessive free play? Do either of you

Since suspensions slowly degrade over time, the owner probably won't notice any problems. Have a buddy drive the vehicle while you ride shotgun. He'll be able to spot suspension problems that you can't.
P. Mathiesen

hear small rattles or squeaks? Try to determine the exact location of any noise. Under the truck, does anything appear to be loose? Grab the steering components (tie rods, steering links, and Pitman arm) and give each a good yank. Slight free play—the result of normal wear and tear—is acceptable, but anything more means a trip to the shop. (For our purposes, "slight" is defined as .030 inch, the width of a standard paper clip.)

2. Have your friend turn the steering wheel all the way to each side. You're now listening for big noises: groans, creaks, and the like. As your friend turns the wheel, your eyes are glued to the major suspension mounting points. Depending on the model, these include ball joints, king pins, control arm bushings, and leading or trailing arm bushings. Track down the source of any noise. The guiding principle here is, "Where there is noise, there is movement, and where there is movement, there are worn or loose parts."

3. The bounce test checks the condition of the shock absorbers and bushings. Have your buddy crouch next to a corner of the vehicle as you push down quickly on the body. The corner should come to a rest quickly; if it continues to bob up and down, the shocks are shot. Groans or creaks heard by your crouching friend are signs of shocks and/or bushings in distress. Either way, get the truck to an expert.

4. Your buddy should run the test drive while you ride shotgun. Have him run the vehicle at highway speeds, and then slowly over a bumpy road. Be alert for shakes in the steering wheel. These could be due to an out-of-balance tire (not serious) or a slowly disintegrating ball joint (big trouble). In an empty parking lot, turn the vehicle in slow circles, first with the wheel

cranked hard right, then hard left. Again, both of you are looking and listening for anything out of the ordinary.

This drill may seem to be a lot of trouble, but it can be done in about 30 minutes. Just don't wait until the night before the deer opener.

DAY-TO-DAY MATTERS

Every year many hunters and fishermen spend hard-earned money on new suspension accessories only to complain about the vehicle's lack of performance. The fundamental mistake is that new components were installed on a vehicle with a worn-out suspension. The problem is difficult to self-diagnose because a suspension slowly loses efficiency over the years. You won't even notice the day-to-day wear.

"When a customer calls, our first question is, 'How old is the truck?'" says Bruce Snyder, marketing manager of Trailmaster Suspension. "We want to know if the ball joints, tie rod ends, and other original-equipment parts—including the springs, bushings, and shock absorbers—are worn-out. You gotta fix those first."

According to Snyder, two of the most important yet overlooked suspension components are bushings and bumpstops. Bushings are

The fundamental mistake that outdoorsmen make when installing new suspension components is that they install them in a vehicle with a worn-out suspension. An older vehicle, such as this Dodge Ramcharger, that has seen a lot of tough miles needs to have the suspension restored to factory specifications before any new parts can be installed.

designed to separate metal parts and absorb the energy created by the motion of the suspension. You'll find them throughout the truck—major locations are leaf springs, shock absorbers, the sway bar and its end links, suspension control arm mounts, and engine and transmission mounts.

"Most people are shocked to find that worn-out bushings can mean a gradual loss of braking and cornering performance, poor steering control under acceleration, and a loss of some shock-absorbing action," Snyder says. "And they fail to appreciate how fast stock bushings can wear out. That's because original-equipment bushings are made of rubber, which is highly susceptible to oil degradation, chemicals, UV rays, salt, and dry rot.

"The ideal replacement bushing is one made from polyurethane. Bushings made from this material will last longer and perform better, and that means your truck will ride and handle better longer."

The bumpstop controls or limits upward suspension travel before it encounters the frame. Bumpstops can be found on control arms, leaf springs, and traction bars. Again, replacing the stock rubber bumpstop with a polyurethane bumpstop will deliver an improvement in longevity and performance.

LOGGING IN

Once the truck has been returned to spec (meaning it now should ride and handle just as it did when it was new), you can evaluate the overall performance of the suspension in regard to accessories or modifications.

"Let's say you want to replace the wheels and tires, which is one of the most common upgrades on 4×4s," Snyder says. "Manufacturers have a broad range of tires—offroad, mud and snow, slick-rock situations, you name it. For best results, you need to match the tires and wheels as closely as possible to the way the truck is used.

"The same holds true for shock absorbers. Shocks really are the personality of the suspension, and like the tires and wheels, should match the way the vehicle is used."

How do you ensure the proper match?

"Many hunters who are serious about their sport maintain a logbook of all their time in the field," Snyder says. "Well, you can do the same thing to document the function of your vehicle. If you record

In order to get the right suspension parts, you need to know exactly how your 4×4 is used. Does it see heavy offroad use? Or is it primarily used for towing? The answer determines precisely which parts are required to deliver the desired ride and handling.

the hours you spend behind the wheel, you'll get a better idea of how the vehicle is really used. You also can make brief notes about the pluses and minuses of the suspension you're currently riding on—things like when it works best and when it doesn't."

The logbook will be an accurate record of the vehicle's *real* use. It will tell you where, when, and how the truck is used. (See the Appendix for a sample logbook.)

With logbook in hand, you can talk knowledgeably about the specific use of the vehicle, which helps suspension experts select the correct accessories. In towing applications, for example, the biggest consideration is stability and load-carrying capacity. The components that Trailmaster would recommend for a truck used in this manner are different from what the company would suggest for a slick-rock offroad application. Likewise, a purpose-built hunting and fishing vehicle that will spend most of the time offroad requires a different setup from a pickup or sport utility that is used by multiple family members for work and sport.

Keep the log in the glove compartment or console where it's handy. And clip a pen to the front cover, so you'll use it.

PART 2: THE SOFT MACHINE

IS THE TRUCK of today too soft? Many hunters and fishermen think so. Let's look at the situation a friend of mine encountered with his late-model Suburban. Doug is an avid waterfowler, big-game hunter, and fisherman who tends to push his truck to the limit. He's been bogged down in a South Dakota cornfield while goose hunting,

This Suburban was fitted with premium shock absorbers and auxiliary air springs to help improve trailer-towing and load-hauling performance.
P. Mathiesen

buried in a Nebraska mudhole while deer hunting, and high-centered on a remote Missouri trail while trout fishing. Though most of his towing is done with a small boat, he occasionally tows bigger loads. He is also a gear freak of the first order—which means he tends to overload the truck with all manner of hunting and fishing equipment.

"My frustration is that I picked a ³/₄-ton Suburban so I would have extra load-carrying capability," Doug told me. "But the rear of the truck sags noticeably when it's fully loaded. And under heavy braking, the nose really dives. What's going on?"

Welcome to the world of the modern truck. There was a time (back when television cowboys Roy Rogers, Gene Autry, and Hopalong Cassidy ruled the range) when the sport utility was viewed primarily as a work vehicle. It had a Spartan interior, three-speed transmission, and stiff leaf springs fore and aft designed to handle massive loads. The ride wasn't pretty, but that was the nature of the beast.

These days we ask SUVs and pickups to do much more. The new breed of SUV/pickup owner expects passenger car comforts—that's why SUVs come with plush interiors, comfy seats, and a ride like grandfather's Fleetwood. Fine. But that trend leaves hunters and fishermen who drive offroad or tow heavy loads stuck in the middle. By "softening" the modern truck suspension to meet the requirements of new owners, manufacturers have compromised load-carrying capability for those of us who really need it.

Given the kind of performance Doug required of his Suburban, I recommended a suspension upgrade. First, he replaced the original equipment shocks with premium shocks, which utilized a sophisticated design that improved the shocks' ability to respond quickly and efficiently to widely differing driving conditions.

"Though shocks are often considered solely in the context of ride quality, they have an equally important role in traction and steering control," says Snyder of Trailmaster. "By helping to maintain proper tire-to-road contact, a shock helps improve traction, steering response, and braking effectiveness."

We opted for a quality shock to get that performance and to ensure it would mate well with the second part of the installation— auxiliary air springs.

Air springs are primarily load-leveling tools. This is a key role; a vehicle that is not level will not handle properly. By restoring the vehicle to level ride height, air springs also help ensure that the stock steel springs and the shocks work in optimum conditions.

Air springs, available for leaf- and coil-spring applications, use compressed air to inflate and deflate an air bladder to achieve the desired ride height. The controls are mounted in the cab for easy operation.

On the coil-spring application, a polyurethane cylinder is inserted into the spring and a feeder hose for the air is inserted into the top of the bladder. The springs can deliver 1,000 pounds of leveling capacity per pair.

There are two types of leaf-spring applications, sleeve and bellows, each of which is constructed of fabric-reinforced rubber, much like a tire. The sleeve type delivers up to 2,500 pounds of leveling capacity per pair. The bellows unit is heavy-duty: It can handle up to 5,000 pounds of leveling capacity per pair. (Air springs are not available for trucks equipped with torsion bars.) Never exceed the manufacturer's Gross Vehicle Weight Rating (GVWR), which can be found in the owner's manual. GVWR is the combined weight of the vehicle, passengers, and payload (your gear).

"Air springs help deliver the versatility that today's truck owner demands. The system gives you the capability to fine-tune the ride under widely differing road and load characteristics, and it also makes for a more comfortable ride and better handling," says Snyder.

Doug has had the system in his Suburban for a year now, and he remains impressed with how his truck handles, both on and off the road, loaded and unloaded. "What a difference," he said. "Sway and nose dive? Gone. They simply disappeared once I had this system in place. Last summer I drove to Canada to fish with four buddies. We filled the back of the Suburban to the headliner with camping and fishing gear. We even maxed out the roof rack. But the truck handled fine during the whole trip.

"With this setup, I feel like I can have my cake and eat it, too." And that says it all.

BALANCING ACT

When considering any kind of shock and auxiliary air-spring upgrade, keep in mind the concept of balance. You want to match the springs and shocks as closely as possible. Matching light-rate springs with heavy-control shocks is a recipe for disaster.

The tough part is that what works for one type of truck (and owner) may not work for another. The way a truck is used, the speeds at which it is operated, the loads it is required to carry, and the surfaces over which it is typically driven are critical factors in determining balance. That's why you should consult with a reputable suspension outfit before you buy any aftermarket components.

INSTALLATION NOTES

If you do a lot of heavy-duty offroading, make sure you tell the auxiliary air-spring installer. He needs to know so he can route and tuck away the air lines to keep them away from offroad obstacles. For our Suburban, the installer ran the lines next to the vehicle's hydraulic lines and then tied off the lines every 10 inches to guard against sag. Also make sure that the air lines don't touch hot exhaust parts. Finally, place the fuse for the air compressor in an accessible spot. If you are offroad and damage a line or bag, you'll need to pop the fuse to shut off the compressor. If you don't, the air compressor will continue to pump—and that will eventually drain the vehicle battery.

PART 3: UPLIFTING STORY

JIM AND I ran into the 7-11 outside El Dorado, Kansas, for hot coffee and a box of powdered-sugar doughnuts—the essentials required to ward off the chill of a late-autumn pheasant hunt. Outside a kid in camo was standing in front of his new 4×4, which drew admiring stares because of its monster truck lift.

"Nice job," I said. "But how does this thing perform offroad? It seems a little top heavy to me."

Lift kits are a popular option, but in many cases truck owners lift their vehicle too high, which compromises the 4×4's performance. This compact pickup was lifted 2 inches, which provides improved ground clearance for offroading without degrading ride or handling.
E. Stewart

"Oh, I had to disconnect the four-wheel drive when I did the lift," he said. "Major bummer, but it was the only way I could get the lift I wanted."

"In that case, why didn't you just buy a two-wheel drive?"

He looked at me as if I had just fallen off the turnip truck. "Are you kidding? Around here, man, four-wheel rules."

Although the average outdoorsman isn't searching for a monster lift look, he no doubt realizes the value of a modest lift that can deliver precious inches in ground clearance. It can also allow the installation of beefier tires, for show or go. But be careful. In too many cases a guy can act like our Kansas kid and end up with a 4×4 that can't do the job.

Here's how: Let's say you opt for a 4-inch lift kit and then throw on a set of 35×12.50R16.5 mud-terrain tires with larger diameter wheels. In this case, you're asking for trouble because you—like Junior—didn't bother to match the new components to the limitations of the truck's suspension.

"Think about it," says Snyder of Trailmaster. "If the truck came with original-equipment LT235/75R15 tires, the outside diameter of those tires is 29.1 inches. The wheel is 15 inches in diameter. The truck manufacturer took those dimensions into account when the truck was built. All of the suspension components are designed to work in concert with those numbers, including how the tires fit in the wheel wells.

"But now you have 35-inch mudders, which have an outside diameter of 35 inches. The new wheels have a diameter of 16.5 inches. Do the math. A 4-inch lift kit will leave you 2 inches short in the wheel wells—and I'm only talking about the tires.

"What about the brake lines, hoses, and wiring? In addition, you've also moved the axle farther from the frame. Don't tell me that

A matched lift system from one manufacturer and specifically designed for your vehicle is the best way to go. That way you get all the hardware, brackets, and shocks in one package.
E. Stewart

won't affect performance. What about control arms, shocks, and all of the rest?

"My point is that you need to ask a lot of questions before you start. The good news is that the aftermarket has come up with plenty of answers."

Bottom line: You want a lift kit that contains all the right pieces, and each part should be specifically designed to fit your vehicle. For example, Trailmaster has 50 suspension kits (in 2-, 4-, and 6-inch lift configurations) designed to match a wide variety of domestic makes, including Jeep, Chevy, Ford, and Dodge.

"Our 4-inch lift kit for the Chevy Silverado and GMC Sierra $1/2$-ton 4×4 pickups provides 4 inches of mechanical lift by lowering all factory suspension mounting points," Snyder continues. "Included in this system are replacement crossmembers, which connect driver and passenger side lower control arm brackets, replacement tubular-style upper control arms with greasable polyurethane bushings, and premium ball joints with grease fittings."

The kits also include new center drag link and tie rod extensions, differential drop brackets, a two-piece front skid pad assembly, heat-treated hardened and plated upper ball joint spacers, torsion bar drop brackets, and all the necessary hardware needed for installation. That's what I mean by complete.

SHOCKING ADVICE

One of the most common upgrades is shock absorbers. Here are some tips to follow when changing them.

- Get rid of the stock shock. If you bought the vehicle used, the shocks are shot. Changing the shocks is especially important if you invest in tires and wheels—which aren't cheap. If you don't upgrade the shocks as well, the tires may wear out prematurely.

- A shock absorber expert once told me, "Valving is what sets a good shock apart from a poor shock. With proper valving, the wheel doesn't hop and bounce. More durable shocks also feature a larger shaft, with a larger oil reservoir. This helps prevent overheating, a typical problem with cheap shocks. When a shock absorber overheats, the oil foams, which prevents the unit from being able to rebound properly. The wheels will start bouncing all over the place, and you won't know what's going on. The next morning you take it to the shop, but they can't find anything wrong. That's because the shocks have cooled off and the foaming has ceased."

Picking the Right Tire

*If you can count to four, you can pick
the correct tire for your 4×4.*

IT DIDN'T TAKE me very long to learn how to tell a brown trout from a rainbow or brookie. And I easily mastered the differences between a pumpkinseed and a bluegill. But when confronted with the redear, redbreast, or longear sunfish, things got a good deal more complicated. Even now, I occasionally consult a field guide to be sure.

So it is with tires for a 4×4. With so many designs available, how can you identify the correct tire for your pickup or sport utility? Consulting the simplified "field guide" below can make things easier. Use it to narrow the choice to a particular type of tire. Then go to a dealer for information on the specific model within that tire type.

Essentially, there are four types of tires of concern to outdoorsmen: 1. highway rib; 2. highway/all-season; 3. offroad/all-terrain; and 4. maximum-traction offroad.

1. Highway rib tires are most commonly used in commercial applications. (A rib is the standing tread that circles the tire.) The design provides good, even wear, low noise levels, and a smooth ride. Highway rib tires usually have a four- or five-rib design. Each rib is siped, which means the ribs have little slashes that help provide biting edges for traction in dirt, slush, and snow. The grooves between the ribs can be jagged to provide even more of a bite. The shoulders (the inner and outer ribs) are wider to help cornering and braking performance. These

Highway rib

38

tires are designed primarily for highway use, but will perform adequately in light to moderate snow and on level gravel and dirt roads.

2. For the most part, unless you specify an offroad tire option, highway all-season tires will probably be original equipment on your 4×4. Sometimes these tires have low rolling resistance, which helps increase fuel economy. The highway/all-season tire maintains the rib-type look, but the ribs consist of small, independent blocks positioned around the tire, which help it deliver greater performance in dirt and rain. The zigzag sipes in the blocks also help traction on snow and ice.

All-season

This type of tire is an evolutionary step up from the highway rib tire. The more aggressive tread design helps it better deal with dirt and snow, so that as loose dirt and snow are compressed into the openings, you actually end up with more traction. At the same time, the all-season design provides good on-road performance. The highway/all-season tire works well on dirt roads, gravel roads, sand, and in moderate snow, and provides a quiet, more comfortable ride.

3. The offroad/all-terrain tire has much more capability off the road. The tire features an interlocking tread design, which means that before the leading tread block leaves the ground, the following tread block has already come into contact with it. This allows the individual blocks to work together to help maintain ride quality and promote even wear. The multifaceted tread blocks also help deliver traction from any direction on dirt, sand, and gravel; provide handling, acceleration, and stopping ability that helps you quickly avoid a rock or a stump; and enable the vehicle to negotiate other obstacles as well. The lugs on the shoulder of the tire and the pockets

All-terrain

between each lug foster good offroad steering response and traction. This is a tire for dirt trails, rocky trails, shallow mud, and moderate to heavy snow; it remains fairly civilized for highway use, though there may be some noise and comfort penalties.

4. As the designation suggests, the maximum-traction offroad tire is focused on offroad travel. Nonetheless, the newest designs can be acceptable for highway travel, though you will experience increased noise levels and potential traction loss in some highway driving situations. Notice that the interlocking tread design now features large, free-standing blocks. Also, the siping has been replaced by large gaps. The goal of this tire is to bite into loose or muddy surface areas for maximum traction and propel the vehicle forward. The very large opening

Maximum-traction

between the lugs helps make the tire self-cleaning: The mud is compressed as the tire gets a grip and is then expelled as the tire rolls on. (Smaller grooves allow the mud to pack in between the lugs and not be expelled.) The wide grooves also help the tire perform well on loose shale and rocks. (Grooves that are too close together can't get a grip, like a rock climber who can't spread his fingers.)

The tire's shoulder area has two designs to further enhance traction on loose or muddy surfaces. The varying shoulder width offers different biting edges for traction, which makes the tire the only choice when you are likely to encounter deep ruts. To take full advantage of this feature, deliberately alternate right and left turns of the steering wheel; this will gently pinch the tire against the edges of deep ruts, which allows the shoulder lugs to claw at the sides of the rut and pull the vehicle forward. In effect, this tactic gives the impression of an additional lower gear. Though it's probably too aggressive for deep sand, the maximum-traction tire is best on loose surfaces, mud, and extremely deep snow.

TIRE TIPS

- Unless you have the luxury of using multiple sets of tires for your 4×4, select a design that meets the worst driving conditions you expect to face. When you're stuck axle deep in mud, you'll forget all about how comfortable your highway rib tires have been.

- When you buy replacement tires, make sure they meet or exceed the original tires' load capacity. Tires that don't will wear out faster and make the truck handle poorly. You also run the risk of tire failure, especially when the vehicle is fully loaded.
- Radial tires dominate the market. There are many reasons for this, but one of the most important is that the design helps the tire envelop an obstruction rather than bounce off it or be punctured. Radial tires are available in each of the tire types presented in this guide.
- Light-truck tires feature beefier construction. Generally, they can handle heavier loads and rougher terrain. Depending on the design, they may ride rougher than passenger-car tires when you drive on the highway.
- Sidewalls are a tire's Achilles' heel. If you routinely venture into terrain with sharp rocks or thorny vegetation that can pierce the sidewall (such damage is not repairable), consider tires built with three-casing plies in the sidewall.
- Be aware that the sophisticated electronic equipment found in modern trucks can be negatively affected by a change in tire size. There is an acceptable range, but if you exceed it your truck's performance may suffer. Consult a knowledgeable tire dealer if you're considering changing tire size.
- A set of good tires isn't cheap. (The range of good tires runs from $400 to $800 depending on the brand, size, and whether you buy them on sale.) Regardless, buy the best tire you can afford. Cheap tires aren't worth the money; they'll wear out faster and perform poorly.

A Question of Size

When many truck owners think about new tires, they often look at new wheels as well. In this case, they often opt for wheels with wide rims, to give the truck a really macho look. Well, wide rims are fine if the truck spends most of its time on pavement, but if you want the truck to be a useful offroad tool, you should actually go with narrower rims, recommended for the specific tire size.

Why? Because the narrower rim causes both beads of the tire to tuck in, which minimizes sidewall exposure. The net result is additional rim and sidewall protection from rocks and other objects that could cause air loss or tire failure. Moreover, the added sidewall flex allows the tire to absorb bumps, resulting in a softer ride.

INFLATION PRESSURES

The number one reason for premature tire failure is improper inflation pressure. For best results, keep the tires at the inflation pressure recommended by the vehicle maker. (You'll find this information in the owner's manual.) The pressure branded on the sidewall is the maximum and should be followed only when the vehicle is carrying an extremely heavy load.

There are exceptions to this rule. A common offroad tactic is to reduce tire pressure to improve driving performance. This is ordinarily done when driving over sand, where airing down widens and lengthens the tire's "footprint." Doing so puts more tire in contact with the sand, improving traction. Airing down also works on rocky or stump-studded trails. In this case, the lower inflation pressure allows the tire to wrap itself around a rock, which reduces the chance of a sidewall puncture.

When driving through this type of terrain, impact absorption takes precedence over quick-steering response. For this reason, tire pressures as low as 25 pounds per square inch (psi) may be used, so long as speeds are less than 15 mph.

Be sure the tire has adequate load-carrying capacity at these lower pressures. To be safe, don't go below 18 psi. The disadvantage to airing down is that you increase the probability of pushing a tire off the rim. Be alert.

Always make sure the tires are returned to the proper inflation pressures before you return to the highway. Severe internal tire dam-

Reducing tire inflation pressure helps improve offroad performance when driving over sand, rocks, or stump-studded trails.
E. Stewart

New tires or not, trouble will always find you if you don't pay attention to the trail. It's better to rely on common sense, rather than technology, to get you out of a jam.

age or outright failure can occur when an underinflated tire is driven at typical highway speeds.

DRIVING TIPS

Joe and I had parked the 4×4 at a small pullout next to the public access area and were uncasing our shotguns. The road in was ravaged; it was full of nasty ruts and gravel mounds, and the last 100 yards were especially treacherous because it dropped so steeply. As I slipped on my game vest, I heard the sound of another engine, and when I looked up I could see the driver was having trouble coming down the trail.

"Joe," I yelled. "Get out of the way!"

Joe leaped behind our truck as the vehicle careened by and bounced off a huge tree. Fortunately, the driver wasn't hurt, but his new truck had a nasty dent in the front quarter panel. He climbed out and said, "Sorry, boys. Didn't mean to make you jump like that. I don't understand it. I just put new offroad tires on this thing."

New tires or not, if you don't pay attention to the trail, trouble will always find you. Later, when I stopped by to talk with Steve White, light-truck tire marketing manager at Uniroyal, and tell him the story, he said, "That guy made a classic mistake. He relied on technology rather than common sense to get him out of trouble."

"Yeah," I said, "I see that a lot."

"What people forget," White said, "is that good tires are only part of the package. You also need to hone your offroad driving skills. And you begin with equipment every driver already has."

"And that would be?"

"Your eyes. You need to know what to do with your eyes. Too

Always make sure the tires are returned to the proper inflation pressures before you return to the highway. The only way you can do this is to invest in a good tire pressure gauge.
E. Stewart

many people simply stare straight ahead, focusing only on what is immediately in front of the vehicle. Wrong! You should be using your eyes to gather much more information. For instance, what's on each side of the truck? Are there sharp rocks or overhanging tree limbs? What about cactus? You need to know this. Take a look down the trail. What's coming up? Deep ruts, a blind turn? Do you have an obstacle that you need to steer around? Or can you drive over it? You need to know this too, so trail challenges don't come as a surprise.

"Always try to keep in mind what I call 'the picture,' which I define as where I want the truck to *go,* not where it currently *is.* That's a big difference, but if you can do it, you'll avoid a lot of trouble.

"In order to see 'the picture,' you need to be seated comfortably in the vehicle. You shouldn't have to strain to reach the pedals or steering wheel, and you should be able to clearly see the gauges as well as the mirrors. Drivers who aren't comfortable will get fatigued, and this affects your ability to control the vehicle."

The next step, according to White, is to drive the vehicle with the correct speed and rhythm. When you get it right, you should be able to hold a full cup of water without spilling it as you drive.

"You need to learn how to accelerate properly," he continued. "Too many offroaders employ a herky-jerky on- and off-throttle type of driving. This only upsets the balance of the vehicle. Instead, gently accelerate to a level where you can keep relatively steady pressure on the accelerator. Make only subtle adjustments to slow down or speed up.

"Do all of your braking before you get to a turn, hole, or whatever it is that is forcing you to slow the vehicle. Remember, your brakes are going to be a lot more sensitive to locking up in dirt or sand

One of the major problems when driving offroad is excess speed. In many cases, drivers are not aware of vehicle speed, and most are going faster than they think.

because the tires have less traction. Make the braking action as subtle and as smooth as possible. If you do encounter a crisis, brake hard—just to the point of lockup. At that point, gently ease off the brakes in small increments to allow the tires to maintain traction, but keep enough pressure on the pedal to continue to slow down the vehicle. Once the vehicle starts to skid, you may have a tough time trying to recover because offroad situations can have minimal traction to begin with.

"Obviously, the slower you're going when you get in a panic situation, the easier it will be to deal with. In fact, one of the major difficulties in trying to execute turns in offroad situations is excess speed. In many cases, the driver is not aware of vehicle speed—and most drivers are going much faster than they think. When that happens, you'll find that the truck wants to keep going straight ahead rather than turn in the direction you are steering.

"That's what I call a skid," I said.

"Right. And it's trouble, so slow down."

Rolling Along

There's more to wheels than meets the eye.

THE HAND-DRAWN map was pinched between my thumb and the steering wheel. According to the smeared lines, I would be able to see the river after the next curve. I had been told that the pullout overlooked a great stretch of pocket water. "Big 'bows," my friend had said over the phone. "Even better, almost no one fishes this stretch."

"Why?" I asked.

"The road is really in miserable shape. A lot of it washed out last winter. Take it slow."

The road was bad, but when I made the pullout there was one fellow ahead of me. He was shucking his waders as I pulled in.

He nodded, stowed his rod, and then ambled over to talk. "Nice-looking wheels," he said. Then he bent down for a closer inspection. "Aluminum?"

I nodded.

He spat a long stream of tobacco juice. "Don't care for it. I want a strong wheel. Steel for me."

STRESSFUL MATTERS

Like most outdoorsmen, this guy didn't beat around the bush when it came to opinions on gear. And he certainly wasn't the first who questioned the wisdom of tackling tough offroad trails on aluminum wheels.

When I got home I tracked down Laurie Simpson, staff product engineer at Alcoa Wheel Products International, and asked her, "Look, I haven't had any trouble with these wheels, but boy, do I catch it when other guys learn I'm driving on aluminum. What gives?"

I could hear Simpson take a deep breath. Obviously, this was a familiar question. "The aluminum forged wheel manufactured by Alcoa is actually stronger and tougher than a steel wheel," she told me. "The other goodie is that our wheel is about half as heavy as steel. And a lighter wheel gives the vehicle better handling characteristics.

"What many of your guys don't know is that there are actually three types of aluminum wheels on the market—cast, billet, and forged. Each process leaves the product with certain traits as distinctive as fingerprints."

That brought us to a technical discussion on metallurgy—not my field. Boiled down, Simpson said that a cast wheel is produced by pouring hot molten metal into a die. The process creates little air pockets, which can lead to "fatigue cracks that can reduce the strength and performance of the wheel."

The way to solve that is to create a heavier wheel in which cracks take longer to form. That's why cast-aluminum wheels can weigh as much as 20 pounds more than a forged aluminum wheel. (Steel wheels, by the way, can weigh as much as 30 pounds more than a forged aluminum wheel.) The extra weight, however, can compromise handling. In this case, heavier is not better.

The rolling process that creates billet wheels help eliminate the porosity problem, but the process requires the manufacturer to build a two-piece wheel—a machined billet center welded or bolted to an outer rim. The weakness here is the strength of the weld that holds the two sections together.

Forged wheels, on the other hand, have no air pockets. Solid alu-

While many new trucks now come from the factory with better-built aluminum, rather than steel, wheels, new aftermarket aluminum wheels are one of the first changes an outdoorsman makes to his vehicle.

minum is heated, compressed, and formed into the shape of a wheel—a process that eliminates the pores that can lead to cracks. One-piece forging also aligns the grain flow of the metal, which significantly improves strength and durability. All of this means that the wheel is less likely to fail in tough offroad situations. The wheel may bend, but it won't break.

And steel? The problem with steel wheels is that two separate welding operations are required: one to form the rolled rim, another to attach the center disc. Welds concentrate stress, and where stress is concentrated, failure gets an opportunity to do its worst.

GOING TO EXTREMES

I next asked Simpson to give me an example of how tough forged wheels really were.

"Easy," she said. "The Ford Rough Rider offroad racing team has been on Alcoa forged wheels for the past four years. They've had more than 30,000 miles of desert racing without a single wheel failure. In the past, it's been common to change a wheel three or four times in one event."

"What has desert racing got to do with hunting and fishing?" I asked.

"Actually, a great deal. Offroad racing teaches us what can go wrong in extreme situations, which gives us the opportunity to make a good lightweight product for guys who hunt and fish in tough terrain.

"Most people don't think weight savings is important, but it is," Simpson said. "Lighter wheels improve handling, especially when you're offroad. The less weight you have bouncing up and down underneath that spring, the easier the vehicle is to control.

"And as long as we're talking ride, keep in mind that forged wheels ride better with less vibration. The design helps eliminate brake shudder and excess tire wear."

To put the matter totally to rest, I called the owner of a truck conversion center, who said, "In all the years I've been installing forged wheels, not one has been returned because of breakage. I think a major reason is the one-piece design. Two-piece wheels, which are also known as fabricated wheels, regardless of construction, don't seem to fare as well over the long run in 4×4 applications."

As for my tobacco-squirting friend, he no doubt recalls the debate that raged among hunters and fishermen a generation ago when aluminum wheels first made large inroads in the aftermarket offroad wheel market. There were some quality issues, but those were put to bed a long time ago. In fact, many trucks come out of the factory with stock aluminum wheels.

So, the big question: Should you buy cast, billet, or forged wheels? Forged wheels are the best overall choice, but however you decide to go, buy the best wheels you can afford. Cheap wheels, like cheap tackle, won't cut it.

LOOKING GOOD

Outdoorsmen want a rugged wheel, but they also want to improve the appearance of their 4×4. An advantage of the forged aluminum wheel is that its bright chromelike appearance requires little maintenance. There is no paint to chip or flake off, and the wheel won't rust—definitely a problem with steel.

"Although many companies use a conventional clear coating to help protect the appearance of the wheel, Alcoa does not," says Simpson. Why? "Because the coating can be damaged in certain applications, which degrades the overall look of the wheel. With our wheels, all you need to do to keep them looking good is a seasonal wash and polish.

"The wheels may not help you catch more fish," Simpson said before signing off. "But they'll look good. And they certainly will get you where you want to go—and get you home again."

"THE FOUR HORSEMEN"

Let's say you've got your eye on a set of smart-looking aftermarket wheels. What's next? You need to make sure the wheels will fit your vehicle. This is a bit complicated, but if you follow the guidelines below you should end up with wheels that do the job.

Four characteristics determine wheel fit. They are: 1. size (wheel diameter and rim width); 2. bolt circle; 3. load rating; and 4. offset. Let's look at each in turn.

1. Size: Select a wheel size appropriate for the desired tire and

Every wheel has a number of evenly spaced bolt holes. Some truck wheels have eight bolt holes (typically, full-size models), while others have five bolt holes (typically, compacts). You need to make sure that the bolt holes on the wheel you're interested in match the studs on your truck
E. Stewart

load-carrying capacity. A given tire size can fit a range of rim widths; in other words, a P265/75R15 tire can be used on a 7- to 9.5-inch wide rim. The rim width will affect the appearance of the tire by changing the sidewall profile.

2. Bolt Circle: A wheel has a number of evenly spaced stud or bolt holes. The bolt circle is the diameter of an imaginary circle that runs through the bolt hole centers. You measure from the center of one bolt hole, across the center of the hub face, to a point that intersects the imaginary circle drawn through the bolt hole centers. This measurement is usually stated in inches or millimeters.

3. Load Rating: The maximum load rating of the tire, wheel, and axle must be compatible. A bigger wheel does not always mean a bigger load rating. For example, several Alcoa 16×7J wheels carry maximum load ratings of 2,600 pounds, yet other Alcoa wheels the same size are load-rated to 3,040 pounds. The load rating on your new customized equipment should be at least as high as the original equipment wheel and tire.

4. Offset: Of the four fitment characteristics, this is by far the most complex. Offset is the distance from the wheel mounting surface (mounting pad) to the centerline of the rim. Zero offset means the rim centerline is in line with the mounting surface. Negative offset means the centerline is outboard of the mounting surface; positive offset means the centerline is inboard of

Make sure the new wheels and tires will fit your truck. Looks can be deceiving. Though the wheels and tires on this Ford F250 look small, they're a perfect fit. The reason the combo looks small is that the 4-inch suspension lift has raised the wheel well above the wheel and tire.
E. Stewart

Although this wheel and tire combo looks fine, both the wheels and the tires are actually a shade too large for the truck, which causes the tires to scrub the wheel wells. That's why you should have the wheels and tires pre-fitted at a shop before you buy.
E. Stewart

the mounting surface. Changing offset too much from stock may accelerate tire wear, impede steering response, and hamper stability.

"It's a good idea to match the original equipment wheel backspace when going to wider tires. This helps prevent fitment problems," Simpson says. "Getting the right offset for your particular application is 90 percent of successful custom wheel fitment. Offset is crucial to avoid clearance problems with fenders, struts, anti-sway bars, brake calipers, and other suspension parts. Maintain the wheel offset as close to stock as possible, especially on the front wheels."

SIX STEPS TO SUCCESS

Simpson recommends a six-step procedure that any professional installer can do for you. Following this guide will ensure that the new wheels fit the tires and that the new wheel-tire combination fits the truck.

1. Place the truck on a lift rack and raise it off the floor. Remove one front wheel.
2. Clean the mounting surface on the hub with a wire brush and remove any retainer (spring) clips.
3. Hold the aftermarket wheel (no tire) on the hub and check for a flush mount. The mounting surface of the wheel must fit flush to the hub mounting surface. The back side of the wheel must not rest against any obstructions such as the brake caliper, suspension components, balance weights, or rivets.
4. Install three lug nuts and hand-tighten. Rotate the wheel and fully turn the steering wheel in both directions to ensure complete clearance.
5. Repeat the above steps on the rear of the vehicle. (The one exception is that you won't need to turn the steering wheel.)
6. Finally, mount the tires to the new wheels and install all four on the truck. Lower the truck to the floor. This will put the vehicle in a "true" ride position because the weight of the truck will settle on the tires, causing them to spread closer to underbody components. Make sure tires and wheels aren't in contact with suspension or other components.

When Big Isn't Best

Sometimes, it pays to think small.

NO GOOD DEED ever goes unpunished. That's what I was thinking while a deer-hunting buddy was giving me a thorough tongue lashing one evening. I had recommended a new set of aggressive-tread offroad tires for his 4×4. He had acted on my advice, and then promptly sank his truck in thick mud while scouting a new hunting area.

"You know how much that tow operator charged me, pal? He put the hurt on me but good. And those new tires and wheels? They cost me a bundle—and the mud just ate 'em alive!"

Wheels? I didn't talk wheels with him.

"Did you buy wheels, too?" I asked.

"Had to. The old ones wouldn't fit the new tires."

"Did you buy *bigger* tires?"

"Of course. I really wanted monster mud grabbers."

"How big?"

"Big!"

Now I knew the problem. "Did you change the gears as well?"

"What are you talking about?"

BIG PROBLEM

What my friend experienced is one of the most common and bedeviling problems faced by anyone who hunts and fishes out of a 4×4. If you replace the original wheels and tires with larger units, you also need to change the gears.

New tires and wheels are one of the first changes made to a new truck. There's just one problem . . . if you buy bigger tires, you'll need to change the differential gears as well.
E. Stewart

When my blistered ears had cooled down, I got in touch with Jonathan Spiegel, co-proprietor of The Progress Group, a California-based company that specializes in light-truck custom performance. He had modified a Ford F250 pickup for me by replacing the original-equipment ring and pinion gears with high-performance components designed to stand up to heavy offroad use and to provide greater pulling power. He seemed to be the perfect guy to help explain gears and gear ratios.

"Gear ratios greatly effect how well a truck performs in hunting and fishing situations. Even so, they are largely overlooked, probably because the gears are hidden in the rear differential housing," he told me.

"Well, all I know is that my modified F250 had much more pep in low-rpm high-torque situations, just what was needed to keep the vehicle moving in muddy offroad conditions," I said.

"I'll try to make this as simple as possible," Spiegel said. "Gear talk can get really complicated—all right, downright boring—which is why so many sportsmen just tune out when guys like me start talking."

"Well, where do we start?" I ask. "The ring or pinion gears? The differential housing? Spider gears?"

"Forget that stuff," Spiegel says. "You don't need a technical seminar; you just need to know how gears, in general, affect overall performance. This is what most guys don't grasp. It boils down to a basic understanding of what we call gear ratios."

"And that is. . . ."

"Put simply, gear ratio is a way of matching the power output to the tire size to the desired performance of the vehicle," he says.

"You must be a trout fisherman," I reply. "You make it sound sort of like matching the hatch. There you're picking a fly pattern based on size, color, and silhouette."

Many new trucks come from the factory geared for fuel economy rather than offroad performance, which can create problems when you drive into a muddy cornfield on the way to a deer stand.
P. Mathiesen

Spiegel, who is a complete trout nut, smiled. "Something like that. Let's look at your truck. It had the original factory gear set in it—a 3.54 ratio. In non-technical language, a 3.54 means the driveshaft turns three-and-one-half times for every revolution of the tire. That's a great gear ratio as far as overall driving and fuel economy are concerned, but from a power standpoint it doesn't necessarily give you enough torque."

One contributing factor to the problem is that many trucks now come out of the factory with so-called "high" gear ratios; in other words, gears that deliver fuel economy at the expense of power. Why the emphasis on fuel economy? Because truck manufacturers are under the gun to meet federal fuel economy standards. The problem is that when you run a high gear ratio, the truck may not be able to pull itself out of a mudhole or a boat off a slippery ramp.

"You need to get some power back into that vehicle," Spiegel tells me. "You can't change the engine very easily, but you can change the gear ratio so more torque is applied at the rear wheels. If you lower the gear ratio—for example, go from a three-to-one gear ratio down to four-to-one gear ratio—you've automatically increased the torque available at the rear wheels by 25 percent. That's a significant increase—enough to make the vehicle usable for the intended purpose."

"So, in essence, a gear change can be considered a performance enhancement," I conclude.

"Definitely. Let's go back to your truck. I knew you were interested in using it in offroad situations where you needed the vehicle to crawl at slow speeds with good power. So we changed the gear ratio to a 4.10—four revolutions of the driveshaft for every revolution of the tire."

"Well, that truck was a real monster in the mud," I say. "The only problem was the increase in fuel consumption."

"Yes. When you increase the number of revolutions that the engine turns per minute, you also increase total air and fuel flow. You get more power by using more fuel. So, increasing the gear ratio will increase the fuel consumption. There are always trade-offs in life. You don't get anything for free."

"I also noticed that when we got on the highway and moved up in speed, the truck seemed to hit a wall where it wouldn't go any faster. Is that a factor of the gears?" I ask.

"It's related to the design of the engine and the gear ratio. Engines perform on what we call a torque curve. As the engine rpm starts to increase, the torque output—the available power that comes out of the engine—continually increases until it reaches a maximum point that we call the torque peak.

"When you gear the vehicle to operate beyond the torque peak, the curve starts to fall off; you're no longer in the engine's most efficient operating range."

In other words, for peak truck performance, the gears need to match the intended application.

DOUBLE WHAMMY

"Now we need to relate all this specifically to tire selection," Spiegel says, continuing our conversation.

Tire upgrades are one of the most common changes a truck owner makes. But plenty of hunters and fishermen complain about poor performance after they install larger tires. Here again, gear ratios make an impact.

"As your deer-hunting friend learned the hard way, tire size can actually decrease the performance of the vehicle," Spiegel says. "A larger tire looks good, and it certainly has more flotation area and a greater gripping surface. Going to a wider tire isn't a problem, but if you change the diameter of the tire, you are, in effect, altering the final drive ratio. You'll need to change the gear in direct proportion to the tire size change. If the tire size goes up 10 percent, then you need to change the gear ratio by 10 percent. This way, you'll maintain the same power of the vehicle.

Going to a wider tire isn't a problem, but if you change the diameter of the tire, you are altering the final drive ratio, which has a profound effect on the vehicle's overall performance.
P. Mathiesen

"So moving up to larger tires really does require a change in gears?" I ask.

"Absolutely. Going to a large tire is like trying to pull a boat up the ramp while in high gear. Putting on those large tires essentially has taken away low gear."

Spiegel pauses, hoping no doubt to catch some small indication that I've grasped the basics of what he's talking about.

"So, my buddy's truck probably was geared too high for the kind of offroad driving he was doing," I say. "And going to larger tires only made the problem worse. It's like a double whammy."

Spiegel beams. "Exactly."

"But the problem is also money, isn't it? Gear changes aren't cheap, and they really aren't do-it-yourself jobs."

"No on both counts," he says.

In fact, depending on exactly what is done, expect to pay between $1,000 to $2,000 for a gear change. That may be one reason

Gear changes can run as much as $2,000, which may explain why some outdoorsmen opt not to replace the gears. All that does is condemn the 4×4 to poor performance, especially in challenging offroad conditions.
E. Stewart

why so many of us run for cover when we're told the truck needs a gear change.

And, truth be told, we're probably also prey to the Steak and Sizzle Paradox. We gladly pay for sizzle (macho tires), which can be seen by everyone, but foolishly draw the line at steak (the gears), which are tucked away out of sight.

Well, Spiegel showed me the light. You, too. If you want maximum performance out of your 4×4, pay for the steak as well as the sizzle.

COMING TO TERMS WITH GEAR RATIOS

One of the most confusing aspects of gearing is how gear ratios are expressed. It's an inverse relationship. Low gears, such as a 4.10 to 1, are numerically higher; high gears—2.54 to 1—are numerically lower. Low gears give the truck greater pulling power; higher gears improve fuel economy.

Changing tire sizes and gear ratios may play havoc with the On Board Diagnostic (OBD) system found on late-model trucks. That's because the sophisticated computers that comprise the OBD system monitor a wide range of vehicle functions, including the engine, transmission, and anti-lock brakes. New wheels and gears also will affect the speedometer reading, and when the speedometer, tachometer, and wheel speed readings don't correspond with the pre-programmed conditions in the computer system, the system can get a little testy. Usually a warning light on the dashboard will come on, letting you know that you have offended the sensibilities of the factory engineers; in more serious cases, vehicle performance may be seriously compromised. So before you change wheels or gear ratios

Changing tire sizes and gear ratios on late-model vehicles, such as this Ford Explorer, can play havoc with the truck's sophisticated computer-control system. Check with a good gear shop before you make any modifications.

on a late-model truck, check with an offroad shop that regularly performs these modifications.

Here's an example of what we're talking about.

Let's say you have a stock Ford Explorer with tires that are 28 inches tall and a 2.73 drive gear ratio. At 60 mph, the engine is turning 1,966 rpm. Now add taller tires, say 33-inchers. At 60 mph, the engine will turn only 1,668 rpm, a power loss of nearly 15 percent. You'll notice it immediately; the engine will appear sluggish and fuel economy will suffer.

You can determine your new "effective gear ratio" by using the following formula:

$$\text{ORIGINAL AXLE RATIO} \times \frac{\text{OLD TIRE DIA.}}{\text{NEW TIRE DIA.}} = \text{EFFECTIVE DRIVE GEAR RATIO}$$

$$\text{EXPLORER: } 2.73 \times \frac{(28)}{(33)} = 2.73 \times 8.48 = 2.31$$

As you can see, the increase in tire size changes the effective gear ratio in the Explorer by a considerable amount. To regain the torque lost to the larger diameter tire, you will need to determine what is called the "equivalent gear ratio."

Do the math:

$$\text{ORIGINAL AXLE RATIO} \times \frac{\text{NEW TIRE DIA.}}{\text{OLD TIRE DIA.}} = \text{EQUIVALENT GEAR RATIO}$$

$$\text{EXPLORER: } 2.73 \times \frac{(33)}{(28)} = 2.73 \times 1.17 = 3.19$$

The Explorer needs a gear ratio of 3.19, but the factory gear ratios available for the Explorer (a 4×4 requires you to change front and rear axles) in our range are 3.07 and 3.55. The 3.07s are a bit on the high side, which entails a sacrifice of a small amount of torque for better fuel economy; the 3.55s are on the low side and would be a better choice for offroad use, towing, and hauling heavy loads. The penalty here is higher fuel consumption.

If you don't know your vehicle's drive gear ratio, look at the vehicle specification tag, usually found in the glovebox or on the axle tag attached to the axle cover. You can also check this manually by putting the vehicle on jack stands, blocking the front wheels, and putting the transmission in neutral. Mark the driveshaft and tire with chalk, and rotate the tire one full turn while counting the number of turns the driveshaft makes. This will give you a close estimate. If the driveshaft spins $2^3/_4$ revolutions per 1 revolution of the tire, the truck has a 2.73 ratio. (This procedure will work only if the truck is equipped with a limited-slip or locking differential. If your truck has open differentials—see Chapter 7—you and a partner will need to rotate both rear wheels simultaneously.)

If you don't want to fool with the math, that's okay. Just keep in mind the basic concept: When you change tire size, you'll need to change the gears in order to maintain the performance of the truck.

Locked Tight

Differentials that make a difference.

I T HAPPENS LIKE this: You buy a new four-wheel-drive sport utility or pickup, take it out yonder, and promptly bury it in some mudhole or strand it on a steep talus trail. Now you're in for a really nasty surprise: It can easily cost several hundred dollars to hire a guy to pull the truck free. What gives? The truck is four-wheel-drive, right?

Not necessarily. By design, the majority of stock part-time four-wheel-drive systems don't provide true four-wheel drive. Sure, you get power to the front and rear axles, but the vehicle's standard "open" differential splits that power to the right and left. Doing so

Unless you ordered the optional limited-slip rear differential when you purchased your new 4×4, the vehicle doesn't really have four-wheel drive. With a stock "open" rear differential, all the power is transferred to the wheel that is spinning in mud or on snow and ice. The limited–slip differential shunts a portion of the power to the wheel that has traction, enabling the vehicle to move through most, but not all, obstacles.

allows one wheel to go slower in order for the vehicle to negotiate a corner, but it also shunts all the power to the wheel that's spinning when you get stuck.

Most outdoorsmen have addressed this problem over the years by ordering an optional limited-slip differential for the rear axle. (The option is not normally available for the front axle because it affects steering.) A limited slip is a big help, but as the name implies, the benefits are limited. You may get 40 to 50 percent more traction, but you'll never get full power to both wheels in difficult situations.

POWER SPLIT

What's needed is a full-locking differential, known in some circles as a "locking axle." (Technically it's not, but the result is the same.) Once used only by the hardcore offroad fraternity, the device is beginning to find a new home among more general offroad enthusiasts. One such product is an Australian import—ARB Air Locker. The beauty of this system is that it uses compressed air to lock and unlock the differential. You don't even have to leave the comfort of the cab to engage the mechanism.

According to Jim Jackson, president of ARB USA, "The ARB Air Locker splits the power equally left and right. Now, if a wheel starts to spin, the wheel with traction still gets enough power to keep the vehicle moving."

Jackson says that most outdoorsmen need only to opt for a rear locking axle. "Most people will find that if they just add a locking differential to the rear, they'll be able to deal with 95 percent of all offroad obstacles."

For maximum traction in mud and other sticky offroad situations, locking differentials are the answer.
P. Mathiesen

The extra traction provided by locking differentials is also welcome in towing situations, such as when you attempt to pull a heavy bass boat off a slick ramp.
P. Mathiesen

But if you routinely hunt and fish in country that lies in that last 5 percent, you should consider front and rear lockers. In this case, all four wheels will turn, even if three of them are off the ground. (The fact that the 4×4 is difficult to steer—and well nigh impossible to turn—when both axles are locked is offset by its incredible traction. Once the hard part is out of the way, you can disengage the front or both differentials as needed.)

Another undeniable benefit of a locking differential is that it allows the vehicle to go slower on the trail. "When the wheels are locked, you have a lot more control," Jackson says. "You're not worried about tires spinning. The natural reaction if one wheel starts to spin is to say, 'I'm going to get stuck! I better give it some gas, and get out of here!' But speeding up creates another set of problems. With the Air Locker, you can lock up the axle when you see trouble up ahead and go through that spot slower, with a lot more control and less risk of damage to the vehicle."

Although the installation of a replacement locking differential is not a do-it-yourself job, any good gear or rear-end shop should be able to do it. The job involves taking out the old differential, putting the ring gear from the old differential onto ARB's carrier differential, and re-installing it. There's no serious modification to the vehicle—only the addition of an onboard 12-volt air compressor and air line, which can also be used to inflate tires, mattresses, or float tubes.

"When you activate the system from the controls in the cab," Jackson says, "compressed air goes into the differential and hits a piston attached to a locking gear. That locks one of the side gears inside the case, which locks the two axles together so both turn equally."

You don't have to own a four-wheel-drive truck to take advantage of an Air Locker. In a two-wheel-drive vehicle, if you can fully lock the

The control for the ARB locking differentials is located on the dash. All you do is press to engage (or disengage) the mechanism. You never have to leave the comfort of the cab.
E. Stewart

rear, you will be able to go 95 percent of the places that a standard four-wheel-drive will go.

THE PROOF IS IN THE MUDHOLE

All right, time to put theory into practice. To see whether the system was really up to snuff, I had front and rear locking differentials installed on an F250 pickup in time for deer season. I asked Missouri hunter Peter Mathiesen to find mud worthy of the challenge.

"Let's go to northern Missouri," he said. "The soil there is clay-based; when it gets wet, it produces some really nasty stuff."

The night before our mud test, a fierce line of thundershowers drenched the area. The next morning, Mathiesen told me, "You're gonna find more mud than you can handle, pal."

He wasn't kidding. The first challenge was a steep hill on a dirt farm road. Mathiesen told me the only way to get over the slick rise was to take a running start, "then hold on and hope the mud doesn't send the truck into the ditch."

Another undeniable benefit of a locking differential is that it allows the vehicle to go slower on a trail, especially on muddy hills. Instead of getting a running start, shift into low-range 4WD, lock the differentials, and then crawl—under full control—up the hill.
P. Mathiesen

"Well," I said, "this is different. We'll stop the truck, shift into low-range four-wheel drive, and lock both differentials. Then we'll let the truck crawl up the hill."

Mathiesen just shook his head in awe of my folly. But when the truck proceeded to slowly—and surely—work its way through the mud to the top of the hill, he said, "Okay, it can handle this. I'm impressed. But there's no way it's gonna get out of my mudhole."

"Peter's Mudhole" was a deep trough of slime created where a dirt road crossed a small creek that connected two hayfields near one of our deer stands. To up the ante, I backed the truck in until the front and rear wheels started to spin.

"I think we're in trouble," Mathiesen said. "Come over here and take a look before you do anything else."

When I saw what I had I done, my confidence evaporated. The rear wheels were buried up to the hubs, and the lugs of the tires were completely filled with thick, gooey mud that looked like caramel pudding. The front wheels were in slightly better shape, but they also had lost all traction.

Ford F250 enters a deep mudhole that has snared many a 4×4. Before descending into the hole, the driver has engaged low-range 4WD and has locked both front and rear differentials.
P. Mathiesen

Truck clears the mudhole, though it was dicey going because the wheels were buried up to the hubs.
P. Mathiesen

Rear view of F250, as driver powers out of mudhole. Without locking differentials this truck would have bogged down in mud.
P. Mathiesen

I jumped back into the cab and tried to move the truck. I heard tires spinning and saw mud flying, but the truck didn't budge.

I looked at Mathiesen, who said, "I'd laugh except that it's a long walk out."

Well, I had one more ploy. I rocked the truck slightly, then felt the front tires grab traction. And with that, the pickup broke free and rolled out of the hole.

"See?" I told him. "Piece of cake."

"There isn't a 4×4 in camp that could have gotten through that hole," Mathiesen admitted. "I know, because mine had to be pulled out with a winch." He hopped into the cab, kicked giant clots of mud off the soles of his boots, and said, "You proved your point. Now, let's get *Wild Thang* out of here and go get a deer."

GEARING UP

For better offroad performance, I replaced the F250 original-equipment ring and pinion gears with high-performance components specially designed to stand up to heavy offroad use and to provide greater pulling power.

The truck originally had a 3.54 gear ratio, but I opted for a 4.10 gear ratio. (See Chapter 6 for an explanation of gear ratios.) Most times, the gear ratio is changed to compensate for larger offroad tires. My tires really weren't that much larger than stock, but I wanted a lot more low-speed pulling power. The new gear sets gave the truck approximately 16 percent improvement in torque output.

After installation, the gear shop emphasized the need for the offroad outdoorsman to practice preventive maintenance. "Most original equipment manufacturers tell you that you don't really have to do much in the way of maintenance," I was told. "And under normal operating conditions, that's probably true—at least up to 40,000 to 50,000 miles."

But hunters and fishermen don't subject their trucks to "normal" usage.

Say you're backing a vehicle down a ramp to pull a boat out of the water and you back down just far enough to put the rear axle vent tube slightly under water. What happens next creates havoc with the gears. The water cools the warm axle assembly, creating a partial vacuum that sucks water through the vent, where it mixes with the oil.

When that happens, the oil no longer can furnish sufficient lubrication to provide a boundary layer between the pinion and ring gear. As a result, the ring and pinion set are wiped out. You'll lose the bearings, too, because fragments from the deteriorating gear set contaminate the oil and score the bearings.

Bad news all the way around. If you do submerge the axle at a boat ramp, creek crossing, or mudhole, do the following: Remove the differential cover plate as soon as you get a chance and take a close look at the fluid. If the fluid has a milky appearance, it's been contaminated by water and must be changed as quickly as possible. Generally, running the truck 20 to 30 miles isn't so bad; but if you put on more than a couple of hundred miles, you'll damage the gear set as well as the bearings. (If the foregoing is too much bother, stop at a qualified service station and have the mechanic do it for you.)

When you replace the gear oil, use a top-quality product. Going cheap here costs you money in the long run. That's because gear oil not only lubricates and cools working gears, but it is also expected to protect exposed gear teeth and selector fork mechanisms from rust and protect shaft seals and other rubber parts from cracking.

Keeping Transmissions Out of Trouble

Heat kills.

PART 1: HOT ISN'T COOL

I THINK THE VISION an outdoorsman has of a hunting or fishing trip is a lake filled with jumping trout or a big deer stepping out into view at first light. I don't think it's peering under a truck, watching boiling transmission oil pour out onto the ground.

Those are the words of transmission specialist Brian Appelgate of B&M Racing and Performance Products. I've corralled him at a trade show to talk turkey: I want to know how hunters and fishermen can improve the performance of the automatic transmission in their 4×4.

His words surprise me. I was braced for an arcane discourse on clutch packs, control valve bodies, and vacuum modulators.

Appelgate looks at me, smiles, and says, "Now that I've got your attention. . . ." This is a guy used to the thousand-yard stares that transmission talk normally induces. I realize I'm in for something special. So stay with me; you're about to get a painless lesson on how to keep your transmission out of trouble.

COOL SOLUTIONS

"Hunters and fishermen need to know that a transmission will last the life of vehicle—if it's cooled properly," Appelgate says. "Unfortu-

Grinding slowly over offroad trails places a great deal of stress on the transmission.

nately, the way your guys use their trucks—grinding slowly over offroad trails, climbing steep hills, towing boats and trailers—places a great deal of stress on the transmission. Stress creates heat, and heat is the number one killer of automatic transmissions. That's the main reason why so many fail prematurely. But that can be prevented."

How?

"The primary way to control heat is with an auxiliary transmission oil cooler. Any good unit that can circulate transmission fluid efficiently will do the job. And when the fluid stays cool, the transmission enjoys a long life."

I interrupt. "All right. I hear you. But over the years I've talked to many outdoorsmen who believe such equipment really isn't necessary. They say, 'I don't stress the vehicle enough to need one. And besides, the truck comes with a cooler. The dealer's just trying to rip me off for another option.'"

"Yeah. Well, we at B&M for the most part disagree. First, just doing what you guys do—hunting and fishing—stresses the transmission in ways many outdoorsmen don't consider. For example, when you climb a steep offroad trail, you often get a lot of wheelspin, which generates extra heat in the transmission fluid. That's why even though original-equipment transmission radiator technology has come a long way, we still recommend an auxiliary cooler.

"Still not convinced? Think of it this way. It's really no more than an inexpensive insurance policy. Our cooler costs about $60 retail. Compare that to as much as $2,000 for a rebuilt transmission."

Appelgate's eyes have lit up. He's in his element. "In addition, there are a few other things—besides ongoing maintenance, such as changing the fluid and making sure the filter is clean, which many people ignore completely—that anyone can do to increase the life of the transmission.

Wheelspin can generate extra heat in the transmission fluid, enough to overwhelm the vehicle's cooling system.

"Next on the list is to install a deep transmission oil pan. A deep pan allows the transmission to benefit from another 3 to 4 quarts of fluid. If you can circulate a larger quantity of transmission fluid, you greatly increase the ability of the transmission to stay cool."

Though a deeper pan means a small loss in ground clearance, most 4×4s are high enough so the loss doesn't affect offroad performance. It's a worthwhile compromise.

SLIPPING INTO TROUBLE

Appelgate moves over to a cut-away transmission display in the booth. His fingers run over the polished metal surface as if it were the Rosetta Stone. "Heat can also be caused by how the transmission operates internally. Most late-model transmissions are built to be comfortable to the driver even though the shifts may not be most efficient for the transmission. What I mean by this is that some shift overlap and slippage is built in for smooth operation. What we've found, and this is based on years of high-performance transmission experience, is that by improving the quickness and the firmness of the shift just slightly—not enough to be uncomfortable—we can reduce the slippage considerably in the transmission and thereby reduce the heat."

How do you do that?

"The simplest way is to use our do-it-yourself Shift Improver or Transpak valve body recalibration kit. A few simple hand tools and 3 hours of time allow you to modify the hydraulic circuit of the valve body."

None of this alters the status quo of computer controls, so engine performance isn't affected.

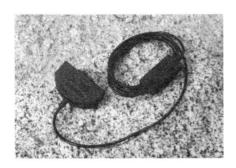

Modern transmissions are built to deliver comfortable shift patterns, but these patterns can create excess slippage, which creates excess heat. A B&M Shift Improver kit helps reduce slippage.
E. Stewart

I ask Appelgate one last question before I leave: "Brian, B&M is really known as a racing company. What have you learned from racing that translates to guys who hunt and fish?"

"Well, actually, it directly relates. By building transmissions for more than 40 years for racing applications, we've found out what all the weak points are. And that helps us improve the breed. Obviously, we don't try to apply everything we learn in racing to a light truck or a hunting and fishing application; nonetheless, a lot of it still applies. It has allowed us to find the most efficient and least expensive ways to cool the transmission."

"Most efficient and least expensive." Now those are words that anyone can understand.

THE BIG FIVE

B&M offers a full line of transmission performance accessories, but five are of particular interest to hunters and fishermen. All are designed for easy do-it-yourself installation.

1. Auxiliary transmission oil cooler. If you want more than 100,000 miles out of your transmission, get one of these. For what it does, it just may be the most inexpensive performance product on the market. ($60)
2. Deep oil pan. In a nutshell—more oil, better cooling. This is a must for 4×4 owners who tow. B&M deep pans also offer a drain plug that allows easier service of the transmission. The pan has a filter extension, which places the filter down toward the bottom of the pan where it can draw in the coolest oil. ($45-$125)

3. Remote Transmission Filter. The other transmission killer is contamination of the fluid. A remote filter makes it easier to access and change the filter. ($30)
4. Temperature Gauge. The optimum operating range of the transmission fluid is between 160° and 200° F. Above that, the fluid starts to lose its lubrication qualities. The B&M gauge is an analog model that displays temperatures from 100° to 350° F. ($45)
5. Valve Body Recalibration Kit. Improves shifts. More important, it helps reduce slippage, which reduces heat. (Shift Improver Kit: $30; Transpak: $55)

PART 2: KING OF THE GRAPEVINE

AS YOU DRIVE along at 65 mph, bass boat in tow, the Lyons Avenue exit on California's Interstate 5 looks like any other freeway interchange. It's home to the usual cookie-cutter cluster of service stations, fast-food restaurants, and convenience stores. You stop, refuel, grab a cup of coffee and maybe a pack or two of Nabs or Devil Dogs. Just like you would any place else.

But Lyons Avenue is different, for just off the freeway you'll find The King of the Grapevine. This monarch doesn't stroll around in a royal purple robe. You'll find him in more common fare, which suits him just fine. This "king" is George Mayer, owner of Mayer's Freeway Shell.

Mayer's kingdom is just down the road from The Grapevine, an infamous stretch of highway that leads to a pair of popular fishing destinations: Castaic and Pyramid lakes. The Grapevine is a torture test supreme for vehicles—36 miles of steep, twisting, mountain grades. Vehicle and towing component manufacturers have learned the hard way that it's a route of no mercy; the notorious gauntlet quickly reveals any flaws in a product's design or execution.

For the past 30 years, tow vehicles stressed to the breaking point by The Grapevine have landed in one of Mayer's service bays, and this hands-on experience has made him a leading expert on towing. During a recent towing test, I stopped at Mayer's station to refuel. While the dual tanks on my diesel tow vehicle drank their fill, Mayer and I talked. His observations are worth noting by anyone who uses a truck or sport utility to tow or haul heavy loads.

WEIGHTY MATTERS

"I think heat is the biggest factor in towing," Mayer tells me. "The vehicle runs too hot."

How do you handle the heat?

"First thing, make sure you have adequate vehicle. Size the vehicle to the load that you're pulling."

In other words, don't try to pull 5,000 pounds with a vehicle rated only for 2,000 pounds. That's a recipe for disaster.

"Next, give yourself a good margin for loading camping, hunting, or fishing gear. The weight of your family or a couple of buddies also needs to be figured in. You have to compensate for the additional load. Most people don't realize how much weight they're adding to the vehicle because they're packing it in a little bit at a time."

Good point. Weight can build up unexpectedly in several ways. Let's take the boat, for example. How did you determine its weight? In all probability, you simply noted a figure in the manufacturer's sales brochure—say, 400 pounds.

But that may reflect only the weight of the hull. By the time you add the engine and other accessories, such as the trailer, you could be dealing with as much as 1,000 pounds.

And don't forget the weight of the fuel (boat and vehicle) or water (in recreational vehicles). Figure about 6 pounds per gallon of gasoline, 8 pounds per gallon of water.

"The best—and easiest—way to determine whether your tow vehicle can handle the load," says Mayer, "is to look up the gross vehicle weight (GVW) in the owner's manual. Hitch up the boat or camping trailer, fill the fuel tanks (on the boat as well as the truck), and load up all the additional gear and people. Then take it to a sand and

One reason many vehicles get into transmission trouble is that the driver doesn't know how much weight the truck is really pulling. All too often, the truck is overweight, which puts a tremendous strain on the transmission.

gravel pit, grain elevator, building and supply company, county waste disposal site, or moving company. These facilities have large drive-on scales, and for a nominal fee you'll get an accurate read on your truck's total weight.

"You do that, you'll know exactly what you're dealing with. I think many people will find that they're overloaded—and that extra weight will kill a vehicle."

Why? Because weight creates heat. And the component that is most vulnerable to heat is the automatic transmission.

HOT STUFF

"Many people don't fully understand how heat fries a transmission," Mayer says. "The transmission will heat up fast while you're towing because the automatic transmission fluid is moving very quickly through it. Heat breaks down ATF, and that leads to premature transmission failure."

Under normal operating conditions, the temperature of the ATF is about 170° F. Stop-and-go traffic can raise the temperature to 250° F—and that's without a towing load. In towing conditions, it's not unusual to get up to 270° F.

"If the temperature gets up to 300° F," Mayer tells me, "you better stop at the next gas station, because you're not going to go much farther than that. You've lost it all."

The easiest and cheapest way to solve this problem is to install an auxiliary transmission oil cooler, which helps ensure that the temperature of the ATF stays in the best operating range. For some reason, many tow vehicle owners resist this option, even though the cost is miniscule ($60 to $120) compared to a rebuilt transmission (as much as $2,000). Another inexpensive transmission-saver is a temperature gauge so you can see when the transmission is headed for trouble.

"I definitely recommend an auxiliary transmission oil cooler," says Mayer. "Remember, the cooler the transmission oil runs, the better. You're definitely going to hit yourself in the wallet if you don't have it.

"I also strongly recommend a drain plug on the automatic transmission—if you can find one. We've learned this from vehicles that get heavy usage. When the transmission oil is drained between filter changes, the transmission is a lot less prone to breakdown and failure."

A gauge that monitors the temperature of the automatic transmission is one of the cheapest and most useful accessories you can install.
E. Stewart

GEARING DOWN

Mayer also believes that The Grapevine claims many vehicles "that are inadequately geared." By this he means that vehicle owners are running the wrong size of differential gears.

Let's say the truck is fitted with a rear-axle ratio of 3.08:1, which is fairly common. This gear ratio ensures good fuel economy but may not deliver enough power to the rear wheels for optimum towing performance. The end result is a lagging engine and a hot transmission—a deadly combination.

But a truck equipped with a lower axle ratio (4.10:1, for example) can pull a load more easily with less heat buildup. This is especially important if your truck pulls heavier loads such as big bass boats. The trade-off is higher fuel consumption, which is still cheaper than rebuilding a transmission (see Chapter 6).

SIMPLE FORMULA

The tanks are full. I'm ready to head up to Castaic to chase bass, but The King is still holding court. So I ask, "George, other than

If the towing vehicle is not equipped with the proper differential gears for towing, performance will lag and the transmission will be put at risk.

transmission work, what's the most common repair you see here?"

"The most common repair we see now is usually related to maintenance. For example, lately we've been seeing a tremendous number of people with pre-1990 carbureted vehicles that are hauling pretty good loads. These vehicles aren't set up for the newer fuels, some of which act as cleaning agents in the fuel tanks. And that can result in plugged fuel filters.

"It's actually pretty preventable if you do regular maintenance. If the filters were changed before the trip. . . ."

"They wouldn't have to make a stop here, would they?" I say.

George smiles. He's seen it all up along The Grapevine.

The intricacies of towing can fill an engineer's notebook with fine print, but for most of us it boils down to a simple formula. If you want maximum towing or load-hauling performance, match the vehicle to the weight, keep the transmission cool, and perform regular routine maintenance. Basic advice. For my money, it's worth a king's ransom.

STOP!

Bringing brakes up to par.

W HEN THE AVERAGE OUTDOORSMAN thinks about enhancing the performance of his 4×4, he often focuses on accessories designed to make the engine perform better. In other words, more power. But for those who load their vehicles to carrying capacity, drive in the mountains, or tow heavy trailers, it's also a good idea to think about better ways to stop.

Factory brakes do a good job within the limits of their design, but sportsmen often push these brakes to the limit, and sometimes beyond. If you've ever experienced brake fade on a steep mountain pass or had a trailer push the truck past a stop sign, you know what I'm talking about. What can you do besides gritting your teeth and gripping the steering wheel?

To find out, I dropped by The Progress Group, a company that specializes in suspension and brake upgrades. The proprietors are a pair of trout-fishing fanatics, Jonathan Spiegel and Jeff Cheechov.

Factory brakes do a good job within the limits of their design, but sportsmen often push the brakes to the limit, and sometimes beyond.
E. Stewart

Larger tires and wheels, one of the most common of all truck upgrades, add weight, and that extra weight makes the brakes work harder. And when brakes work harder, they produce more heat—a big problem.
P. Mathiesen

"When most outdoorsmen decide to modify their truck or sport utility, the last things—if they give them any thought at all—are the brakes," says Spiegel. "This is unfortunate because many modifications directly affect braking system performance. Let me give you an example: The most popular modification is a set of new tires and wheels. Typically, the guy wants larger tires and wheels. Well, that adds weight, and extra weight makes the brakes work harder. And when they work harder, they produce more heat, and then we have a problem."

"Brake pads and shoes are designed to operate properly over a broad range of temperatures," says Cheechov. "But if the brakes get too hot, brake fade can occur. You'll know it when it happens because the pedal starts to feel real firm, and no matter how hard you step on the pedal the truck doesn't want to slow down. It's a real white-knuckle feeling!"

The extra weight and heat created by towing situations can strain brake performance to the breaking point.

According to Spiegel and Cheechov, sportsmen who want to improve brake performance have three options:
1. Increase the friction between the brake pads and rotors (disc brakes) or the shoes and drums (drum brakes).
2. Improve the cooling ability of the brake rotors and drums.
3. Improve your ability to modulate the brakes.

NOT FADE AWAY

The simplest, most common, and least expensive upgrade is to change the brake pads and/or shoes. "For convenience, we'll refer to these items as friction materials," says Spiegel. "Remember, brakes operate by creating friction; if you can increase the friction, you can improve the stopping power."

Typically, such pads cost from $40 to $90 per set. Given how well they perform, they're a bargain. I've driven down steep mountain roads with a 5,000-pound trailer in tow and experienced no brake fade whatsoever. That's a real comforting thought when you crest an 11,000-foot pass.

Technically, friction materials are rated by coefficient of friction (which is nothing more than a "grip" rating), resistance to wear, and reaction to temperature. Different materials exhibit varying degrees of each of these properties. One property noticeable to any driver is "pedal feel." Some materials deliver a smooth, linear feel when the brakes are applied; the truck seems to slow in proportion to the amount of pedal pressure applied. Other materials may feel grabby; at light pressure there is little braking power, but under heavier pressure they grab like all hell. Admittedly, pedal feel is highly subjective,

The simplest and least expensive brake performance improvement is the installation of high-performance brake pads.
E. Stewart

but it definitely affects your comfort level as well as your ability to control the vehicle.

Autospecialty 911 Extreme Performance pads are one example of high-performance pads. They're used in commercial and emergency vehicle fleets for good reason—because the pads offer great stopping power, fade resistance, and good wear characteristics.

Keep in mind that compromises are made when you upgrade pads. Some friction materials have great stopping power, but high wear rates. Others may create lots of brake dust, which means your wheels will get dirty more often. Some materials may not stop well until they are fully warmed up, and some may squeak. Here's where a knowledgeable installer comes into the picture. He not only has the ability to help you select the best friction materials for your particular truck (and part of the country), but he can install them properly.

OTHER OPTIONS

"Upgrading the brake rotors is a more expensive option," says Cheechov, "but the results are worth it, especially if you find yourself in driving situations, such as towing and heavy load hauling, that produce a lot of brake friction and heat."

The most common upgrade is changing to cross-drilled brake rotors, such as those made by PowerStop. These rotors help the front disc brakes dissipate heat more efficiently, which prevents brake fade. An additional benefit of cross-drilled rotors is that the brakes shed water more efficiently, which helps improve stopping power in wet conditions.

Slotted rotors are another option. A slotted rotor has diagonal slots milled into its braking surface. Among other functions, the slots give the brake pads a better bite on the rotor, which helps improve stopping power. The tradeoff is that slotted rotors don't offer the cooling performance of a drilled rotor, and they increase brake pad wear as well. And though both drilled and slotted rotors can be resurfaced, slotted rotors lose their effectiveness when they are machined (or worn) down because the slots lose depth and width. Slotted rotors also don't shed water as well as drilled rotors.

Unfortunately, "high performance" brake drums aren't available. But that doesn't mean you can't do anything. The best bet is to service the brakes and upgrade the rear shoes with heavy-duty friction

Upgrading brake rotors is a more expensive option, but they are worth it, especially in towing and load-hauling situations. Cross-drilled rotors help the front disc brakes dissipate heat more efficiently, which prevents brake fade. The rotors also shed water more effectively, which helps improve stopping power in wet conditions.
E. Stewart

materials, such as PowerStop's "severe duty" types. Also, the outside surface of the drum may be sandblasted to remove rust (heavy corrosion reduces the drum's ability to shed heat). Then paint the drum with a good black high-temperature paint.

Another option is to increase the size of the brake rotors and drums. But tread carefully. You need to learn whether your particular truck has a heavy-duty brake option. (You can do this through a truck dealership.) You also need to talk with a truck expert, because if you opt for larger rotors and drums you'll also need other component parts—calipers, proportioning valve, master cylinder, power booster, and so on. Many brake upgrades require larger diameter wheels and tires, which add substantially to the expense. Buying all this from the dealership gets mighty expensive; if you decide to go this route, a better way may be to scavenge local wrecking yards for the parts. The problem here is that if you're driving an older truck, you may end up buying 20-year-old parts, which may—or may not—be up to the job.

At the top end, you can buy expensive conversion kits that let you replace rear drums with more efficient rear rotors. You can also install a high-end four-disc brake set. The kits do the job, but cost a bundle.

Lastly, you can change the brake lines. Stock brake lines are made of rubber reinforced with woven fabric. As these lines age and are exposed to repeated cycles of high pressure, they tend to become less efficient. Under high pedal pressure, the lines may expand slightly, making the pedal feel soft or spongy.

Aftermarket braided-steel hoses, such as those available from Goodridge, are a cost-effective upgrade that can really improve pedal feel. They can also improve the performance of the vehicle's anti-lock brake system because they remove some of the system's "pulsing." Use only those lines that meet FMVSS 106 (Federal Motor Vehicle

Standards System) and/or Department of Transportation (DOT) standards, and buy lines specifically designed for your truck. Such lines come with proper end fittings and brackets for an exact fit. Avoid lines that require adapters, which are a potential source of leaks.

LOCK UP

In order to stop in a straight line, the front and rear brakes must work in proportion to the amount of weight at each end of the vehicle. If the front brakes are working harder than necessary, for example, braking efficiency is lost because the rear brakes aren't making enough of a contribution. This can lead to front brake lockup, and when that happens you lose steering control. Conversely, if the rear brakes are working more than necessary, the rear wheels can lock up. This creates a situation where the back end of the pickup tries to come around to one side or the other. To counter such problems, truck manufacturers install a proportioning valve to help regulate pressure between the front and rear brakes in order to provide smooth, even braking.

The tendency of the rear of empty pickup trucks to swing around under hard braking led to the creation of the first anti-lock brake systems (ABS) in the late 1970s. At first they were simple mechanical systems that varied the brake pressure to the rear brakes based on the height of the truck bed. When the bed was loaded down the valve allowed more brake line pressure, which increased braking power. If the truck was unloaded, the valve reduced brake line pressure, which reduced the chance of rear brake lockup.

These days most 4×4s come equipped with sophisticated antilock brake systems. But like any new device, there's a learning curve, and many sportsmen—especially those who drive offroad frequently—have reported problems with ABS.

The problem is that ABS were designed to combat slick surfaces. It doesn't take into account what sportsmen encounter: no-traction surfaces. When you reach zero traction—mud, slick rocks, ice—ABS can actually work against you. The lack of any traction doesn't allow ABS to function to its maximum capacity. In practical terms, hunters and fishermen may experience longer stopping distances when braking in offroad situations.

What some offroad drivers have discovered is that in gravel, loose

Though modern anti-lock brake systems (ABS) work well in slick situations, they weren't designed to combat what many offroaders face—no-traction surfaces. The offroad driver would fare better by learning how to modulate the brakes himself rather than rely solely on the anti-lock brakes.
E. Stewart

snow, ice, or mud, the ability to lock the wheel can actually be beneficial. Standing on the brake locks the tire, which allows material to pile up in front of it. And that can actually help bring the vehicle to a faster and safer stop.

It's ironic. The very thing that makes the truck so much safer on the street in inclement weather can cause problems when that vehicle goes offroad.

A major contribution to ABS unease is unfamiliarity with the system. The loud whooshing noise some systems make as the brakes recycle while under full pedal pressure, plus pedal kickback, can cause some drivers to release the pedal prematurely. The solution? Next time it rains, find an empty parking lot. Drive across the lot at 30 mph and completely mash the pedal to the floor. You'll feel the pedal kicking back and hear the noise that's associated with the system. It's a great way to speed up the learning curve.

You can also learn to modulate brake line pressure. "There is still no better computer than the human brain," Spiegel says. "While the vehicle computer has a limited amount of sensors, you have senses of sight, sound, and feeling that the computer doesn't.

"Now, what do I mean by modulation? It's mostly common sense. If the tires begin locking up, ease up on the pedal pressure. Let the tire rotate so you can control the vehicle. Also, maximum braking is achieved by 'squeezing' rather than 'stabbing' the pedal. Stabbing the pedal causes the front of the truck to dive, which causes the rear tires to lose traction and lock up. ABS helps avoid this, but it is not a cure-all. Squeezing the pedal will help the vehicle settle smoothly, which results in a safer stop."

With practice and experience a good driver can actually learn to modulate brakes better than ABS under all but the most slippery conditions. The most important point to remember is this: As long as a wheel is rotating, it tends to travel in the direction it's pointed and will provide maximum traction. When a wheel is locked up, or skidding, it will tend to travel in a straight line and provide less traction. "Properly modulated braking will stop the truck in a much shorter distance than if you just mash the pedal and lock up all four wheels," Spiegel concludes.

This is, admittedly, a tactic for only the most experienced of drivers.

WEIGHT MATTERS

Next time you apply the brakes, pay attention to how the vehicle reacts. The harder you press on the pedal, the more the front end noses down. This is due to a phenomenon known as weight transfer. The more weight transferred forward, the harder the front brakes work. And when you consider that most of the truck's weight is concentrated in front, you now see why the front brakes always wear out faster than the rear. Approximately 65 to 80 percent of the braking power (sometimes more if you brake aggressively) must come from the front brakes in order for the vehicle to stop properly. This is why front-brake upgrades are so critical.

Exhausting Solutions

Breathe in, breathe out.

THE HOLY GRAIL for many hunters and fishermen isn't an in-your-face largemouth that straightens a 2/0 hook or a big whitetail that makes the book. It's a 4×4 with more power. Guys who push a four-wheel-drive pickup or sport utility to the limit by climbing high-mountain offroad trails or horsing a boat and trailer off a steep, muddy boat ramp have learned that modern 4×4s all too often come up a bit short in the power department.

But extra power sometimes comes at a hefty price. A turkey-hunting buddy put it to me point blank: "I want more power, but I don't have the budget or the time for a complete engine overhaul or really expensive accessories. What can I do?"

As it turns out, plenty.

By focusing on the exhaust side of the engine, you can give a 4×4 much more seat-of-the-pants performance at a price you can bear. The reason exhaust modifications can pay off so handsomely is because engine performance boils down to *combustion efficiency*. For an internal combustion engine to make power, it must efficiently convert fuel into heat (power). How well it does this is a measure of its combustion efficiency. Combustion residuals (exhaust gas) that are allowed to remain in the cylinders after each combustion process reduce efficiency, which translates into a loss of power. But if you can rid the engine of exhaust gas faster, you can increase the efficiency of the engine—and that means more power, better fuel economy, and improved driveability. Longer engine life can also result. All in all, pretty good benefits.

By design, the factory exhaust on new 4×4s tends to compromise engine efficiency because the system cannot efficiently expel exhaust gas.

HEAD TO TOE

The greatest gains will come from replacing the engine's stock exhaust manifolds with headers. "Original-equipment exhaust manifolds tend to compromise combustion efficiency, primarily because the factory needs to design vehicles for a very wide range of applications," says Steven Anderson, special-accounts manager for Flowmaster, an aftermarket muffler company. "When it comes to the specific uses that interest your guys—for example, heavy hauling, towing, low-range four-wheel-drive, and high-altitude operation—the factory manifolds can work against you. But aftermarket headers can change that."

What exactly do headers do?

"One of the biggest obstacles to better performance is back pressure, which is the unwanted result of the system's inability to remove sufficient spent gas," says Anderson. "Back pressure causes some of the restriction in exhaust gas flow, as does the design of the stock manifold itself. Typically, a properly designed header is an arrangement of individual pipes that lead from the exhaust ports into a common passage, which eventually enters a muffler. Exact pipe size and length not only help determine how much but where in an engine's rpm range power improvements are provided. Obviously, for trucks it needs to be in the lower range, below 4,500 rpm, where sportsmen need it most."

So, bottom line, headers, when properly tuned, help improve overall combustion efficiency. And that, ultimately, is interpreted as seat-of-the-pants performance. But there's something else as well. Headers can lower the underhood temperature, and that can help extend engine life.

Though some outdoorsmen don't care for the modern "computer" truck, late-model pickups and sport utilities are more dependable than ever, which allows hunters and fishermen to really get to the places that stir their hearts. *P. Mathiesen*

Off-road terrain and conditions vary constantly; you must pay close attention to what is in front as well as what's off to the side, when negotiating any trail. Always keep your brain in gear. *P. Mathiesen*

Though new tires and wheels are the first change most truck owners make, select replacements carefully. Most of us don't need heavy-lugged off-road tires. *P. Mathiesen*

One of the most revolutionary changes in truck performance is the role of the modern computer chip, which allows you to fine-tune engine performance to the tasks at hand, especially off-road driving, load-hauling, and towing. *P. Mathiesen*

A wide variety of truck performance products is now available to suit nearly every outdoorsman's special needs. There's no longer any reason to sit at home and complain about your truck's poor performance. *P. Mathiesen*

Off-road vehicles can benefit greatly from a modest suspension lift, usually in the three- to four-inch range, which helps the vehicle negotiate tough trails without hanging up.
G. Trevor Phillips

This demanding mountain trail is far from any tow service. You'll find that an electric winch will pay for itself the first time it is used. *E. Stewart*

Locking differentials enable a truck to plow through really nasty obstacles such as thick mud. The ARB system on this Ford F250 is operated from the cab. You don't need to step out to activate the differentials. *P. Mathiesen*

Driving in dim light conditions on gravel or other poor traction surfaces is a common problem for outdoorsmen. But an auxiliary light system–in this case from IPF–can really help light the way. *P. Mathiesen*

The best way to get the right aftermarket products is to carefully evaluate how the vehicle is used. Trucks used primarily in off-road situations, such as this Jeep Wrangler, have different needs than a truck used as a tow vehicle. *P. Mathiesen*

This GMC pickup was bought from a utility company. The owner then added a winch, cap, new tires and wheels, and a roof rack to turn it into a real hunting and fishing machine.

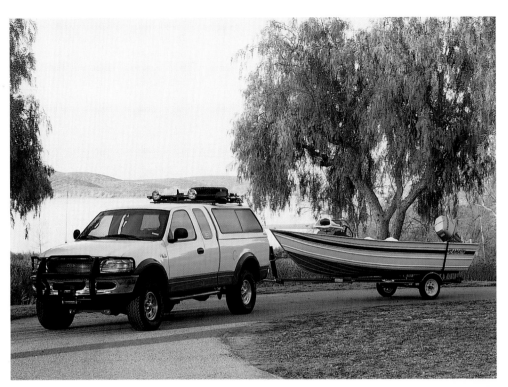

Putting complementary aftermarket products together can pay handsome performance dividends. Here, a Ford F250 benefited from a half-dozen products, including transmission, exhaust, electronic engine controls, and suspension.

An assortment of easy-to-install transmission products, including an auxiliary transmission oil cooler and a high-capacity automatic transmission oil pan, dramatically improved the towing performance of this Dodge Ram 1500.

The addition of high-performance shock absorbers and an auxiliary air spring suspension system improved this Suburban's performance both on and off the road. *P. Mathiesen*

"Cat-back" (catalytic converter to tailpipe) exhaust systems help reduce back pressure, which helps improve overall engine performance.
E. Stewart

"CAT" KITS

For maximum performance, a complete head-to-toe aftermarket exhaust system—headers, catalytic converter, muffler, and tail pipe—is the way to go. A less-expensive option is to retain the stock manifolds, but go with a cat-back (catalytic converter to tailpipe) aftermarket exhaust system. Typically, cat-back systems consist of replacement mufflers and tailpipes designed to reduce back pressure. As a rule, aftermarket cat-back mufflers are a redesign of stock mufflers and are usually found in kit form along with larger-than-stock tail pipes that are specially bent to eliminate kinks or other exhaust-flow restrictions.

Cat-back exhaust systems are designed as stock replacement parts. This is a real advantage for the do-it-yourselfer, as such systems are direct bolt-on equipment that usually retain the factory mounting locations and pipe routing.

A cat-back system is significantly cheaper than a header-to-tail pipe system. Though the rewards are less, the vehicle will still perform better than stock.

NOISE VS. PERFORMANCE

The third and least expensive option is to replace only the muffler.

"As exhaust gas moves from the engine to the tailpipe, it carries a hitchhiker of sorts in the form of sound waves," Anderson says. "The muffler is really a network of baffles that bounce the sound waves around. As they bounce, they cancel each other out; when the waves finally pass out through the tailpipe the sound level has been greatly reduced."

But the price for reduced noise is reduced performance. The typical muffler restricts the flow of exhaust gas, which increases back pressure, which leads to a reduction in engine efficiency and fuel economy. (Note: For the purposes of this discussion, we are not including the catalytic converter, which is another obstacle in the path of exiting exhaust gases. However, federal emissions laws require catalytic converters, so any modification you attempt needs to include the converter.)

"As a rule," says Anderson, "there are three basic types of aftermarket mufflers. The first is intended solely as a stock replacement part. You'll get no performance benefits here. Its obvious asset is its affordability. The second type typically incorporates some form of sound-deadening material—such as fiberglass or steel wool—and an exhaust gas route that is essentially direct or straight through from inlet to outlet. This results in reduced back pressure, which translates into performance gains."

Since type two mufflers rely on the packing material to reduce the exhaust noise, the decibel levels can sometimes rise to annoying levels.

"The third type of aftermarket muffler uses no packing material to deaden exhaust noise," Anderson says. "Rather, it takes advantage of specially placed baffles that have been precisely located to cancel out certain sound frequencies as the sound waves progress through the muffler. In addition, the flow path of the exhaust has been designed to minimize back pressure. Typically, these mufflers, such as those manufactured by Flowmaster, have come out of high-performance and racing environments, but are now beginning to gain wide acceptance among outdoorsmen, especially those who tow boats."

As you can expect, type three mufflers cost more because they do more. And though some truck owners always opt for cost over

Baffle design, as shown in this cutaway of a Flowmaster muffler, helps improve exhaust flow. That, in turn, reduces back pressure and helps deaden exhaust noise.
Flowmaster

Trucks used to tow or haul heavy loads put a big strain on their engines, which increases underhood temperatures. A freer-flowing exhaust system can help the engine shed the excess heat, improving performance.
P. Mathiesen

features, it's best to balance cost, back pressure, and sound control. You may find that by shelling out only a few dollars more, you will get a remarkable improvement in performance.

You may also see performance gains that you didn't expect. "Trucks that are used to tow or haul heavy loads generally place a big strain on their engines," says Anderson. "When these engines work hard, underhood and coolant temperatures rise, and the entire power train becomes more labored. In really bad instances, the temperature may rise high enough to burn spark plug wires.

"Generally, a chronic overheating problem is attacked through the use of oversized radiators, auxiliary transmission fluid coolers, and cooler-running thermostats. Fact is, the problem may be solved, or at least minimized, by a reduction of exhaust gas back pressure. A freer-flowing exhaust not only can help an engine run cooler but can also keep the exhaust gas from choking the engine, and that allows the engine to operate at higher efficiency, especially under towing loads."

As you ponder your options, keep in mind that aftermarket muffler companies such as Flowmaster offer a choice of sounds from quiet to mild to more aggressive tones—all with the same performance gains. So, you can pick the sound you want, though some outdoorsmen—deer and turkey hunters in particular—probably would be better served by a muffler that has been designed to minimize exhaust noise.

CHAPTER 11

Let There Be Light

Seeing is believing.

ISWALLOWED the last of my coffee and said, "Saddle up boy, we got to get in the woods." Then I stepped outside, slipped behind the wheel of my pickup, and cranked up the CD player. At four in the morning, George Jones had his work cut out for him.

Another turkey opener, and we had agreed to meet two other hunters at 4:30. We barreled down the state highway, then turned off onto a farm road. The second the front wheels hit gravel, I reached over and flipped a switch on the dash. Instantly, the road lit up as if I had set off a Roman candle.

"Whoa!" Pete said. "What did you do, supercharge the high beams?"

"Nah. I just added some extra light. I got tired of not being able to see on these country roads."

Modern original-equipment halogen headlights are light-years (literally) ahead of what manufacturers could offer only a few years ago. But they're mass market products designed for average driving conditions. Hunters and fishermen who routinely drive off the road, before dawn and after sunset, and in bad weather, need something more. That "more" is auxiliary lighting.

Auxiliary lighting is designed to supplement the original-equipment headlights. Though the market offers several types of auxiliary lights, for our purposes we're most concerned with driving lamps for long-distance vision, which supplement the high beams, and fog lamps, which supplement the low beams. (The so-called pencil-beam driving light, which has an effective range of 2,000 feet, is a narrow-focus specialty product more suited for offroad desert rac-

Fog lamps are designed to cast light under the fog and illuminate the road or trail sur-
face. Auxiliary driving lamps are designed to supplement your head lights by throwing
light way out in front.
E. Stewart

ing. It doesn't perform well on twisting roads and in hilly and
wooded terrain.)

IN A FOG

Fog lamps are designed to cast light under the fog and illuminate the
road or trail surface. Actually, a better term might be all-weather
lights, since the lamps are also effective in sleet, snow, and dust. The
advantage of fog lamps is their low and wide beam, a result, according to Buddy King, product manager for IPF (a manufacturer of auxiliary lights), "of reflector and lens design. The lens is specially cut to
bend the light down and to the side where it's needed. When the
lamp is properly adjusted, the light won't reflect back to the eye
while driving through rain, snow, fog, or dust.

"A properly aimed fog light is also great for night driving on high-
ways, because the 'cut off' design keeps glare from interfering with
the night vision of oncoming drivers," King notes. "For example, our
ZE-1 light has a vertical spread of only 6 degrees, and when properly
aimed that's well below the line of sight of oncoming traffic."

Fog lamps come in two colors: amber and clear. Clear lenses provide better illumination, while amber lenses are most effective for
glare reduction and depth perception. A rough rule of thumb is "to
see, use clear; to be seen, use amber."

King prefers amber because it produces less glare. "Look for a light that has the gold coating on the glass lens rather than a colored bulb or a yellow-dyed lens," he says. "A colored bulb or lens can diminish the light's intensity by as much as 25 percent. That is why IPF uses a titanium-ceramic coating on the inside of the lens. The coating filters out the blue part of the light spectrum while allowing the red and green portion to pass through without a loss of intensity, producing the amber color."

DRIVE ON

Auxiliary driving lamps are designed to supplement your head lights by throwing light out as far as a half mile in front. "These lights, with a 20- to 30-degree horizontal spread, illuminate both sides of the road," King says. "Essentially, driving lights give you early visual clues about the road ahead and what problems may be out there."

Like deer.

Driving lamps are available in round or rectangular configurations. Choice is largely a matter of aesthetics (many owners prefer auxiliary lamps to match the shape of their 4×4's headlamps). Some light manufacturers claim a rectangular shape provides a broader, better-spread beam, whereas round lights offer better range.

Each state has its own regulations concerning the installation and use of these lights, so check with the appropriate motor vehicle agency before you begin any installation. For example, find out whether the lamps can be wired directly to the regular headlamps and whether they need a separate switch/fuse. You should also know if auxiliary lamps must be covered when not in use and if there are any restrictions regarding the number of forward-facing lights and mounting location.

Experienced offroaders use both types to manage their lighting needs. For example, I use fog lights to improve close-in visibility to gain greater detail of dips, bumps, and rocks. I've also found them invaluable when making U-turns on country roads where ditches line either side. The driving lights break open the darkness beyond the high beams, the best of which are only effective out to about 800 feet. (That's 9 seconds at 60 mph.) Auxiliary driving lights can double that distance, giving you much more time to react to road hazards. In effect, they turn the high beams into a mid-range light, giving you a three-stage lighting system.

Check with your state's regulations concerning installation and use of auxiliary lights. Some states require auxiliary driving lights to be covered when not in use.
P. Mathiesen

MOUNTING PROBLEMS

The majority of fog and driving lights are mounted to the bumper or to a brush guard. Although some owners prefer to mount lights on a roof light bar, truck cap, or tubular roll bars, King advises against this.

"Low-hanging branches will decapitate your high-mounted lights," he says. "In addition, a roof-mounted fog lamp can't do its job. Remember, it's been designed to work low and shoot light under the fog. If it sits up high, you get no benefit.

"High-mounted driving lamps generally cause problems. First, no matter how well designed the lamp is, in this high position it will direct the light onto the hood. And that light gets reflected back to you. Second, the light creates a huge glare problem for oncoming traffic. Lights mounted on the truck cap or a bed-mounted roll bar are even worse; the light comes in through the back window and bounces off the windshield or rear-view mirror.

"However, in certain offroad cases—low-speed trail work or in cornering situations—forward-facing roof-mounted lamps can be very useful."

The closer you can place the auxiliary lights to the headlights, the better. "Automakers always take the prime location to install headlights," King says. "So, placing driving lamps near their headlights is best. That way, the auxiliary lights will deliver better performance. In addition, they will be better protected from hazards, especially if they're mounted in a grille or brush guard.

"Fog lights should be mounted low, preferably just beneath the bumper. Here they will provide the best illumination and the least glare."

The closer you can place the auxiliary lights to the headlights, the better. Truck manufacturers always install headlights at the prime location, so placing driving lamps near the headlights is best.
E. Stewart

LIGHTING MYTHS

Finally, let's dispel a couple of long-standing myths about auxiliary lights. First, it is often said that higher wattage produces brighter lights. "Not so!" says King. "Wattage is a measure of energy over time. It has absolutely nothing to do with illumination. A well-engineered light assembly with a quality 55-watt bulb will provide a more desirable light pattern than an assembly that uses cheap 100-watt bulbs."

Second, some people also believe that lights will overpower a truck's electrical system. "The bigger problem is making sure the installer makes all the connections properly," King says. "This reinforces the desirably of a pre-assembled wiring harness. Poor connections and faulty splices are what draw down the battery.

"Wattage relates to current draw, measured in amperes. To figure the draw on the battery, add the bulb wattage together and divide by the voltage of the vehicle. Here's an example with 55-watt fog lamps. Multiply 55 by 2 to get 110 watts. Now divide 110 watts by 12 volts. The answer is 9 amps—a small load on any alternator."

BUYING TIPS

The current demand for smaller, more aerodynamic lights (a partial result of the smaller frontal area of modern 4×4s) has sparked a revolution in reflector design and bulb technology, allowing manufacturers to build smaller, lighter and, most important, brighter lights. Even so, not all lights are alike. Like so much else in life, you get what you pay for. Given what is at stake, don't go cheap. Buy the best lights you

The best lighting systems come with all components in one package, fully assembled for installation.
IPF

can afford. Here are some points to keep in mind when shopping for lights:

- The best light systems come with all components in one package, fully assembled for installation. Make sure your choice includes the wiring harness, all connectors, switch, and relay in addition to the lights.
- The wiring harness should be fully assembled with high-quality connectors; it should also feature a snap-together weather-proof design that minimizes the chance of corrosion.
- The relays should be high-quality sealed units that resist corrosion.
- Fasteners, including the rivets used in the housing construction, also should be corrosion resistant. Ideally, the fasteners should be made of stainless steel.

12

Helping Hand

Electric winches are always ready to lend a hand.

WHILE FISHING for steelhead on Michigan's Pere Marquette River one spring, I crossed paths with Dan Suman, a steelheader out of Mears, Michigan. When we took a break for coffee, the talk fell naturally to another of Suman's abiding passions—deer hunting. A few minutes later, he said, "Look, I've got a nice piece of woods; why don't you hunt it with me this fall?"

"You bet. Thanks."

"Well, as long as you're here, stop by tomorrow. My sons have just finished building some new stands. That way you can look the spot over. One caution. Though I've bushwhacked a 4×4 trail on reasonably solid ground, the rest of the place is a total bog. You need to be *real* careful driving in."

"No problem," I said. "My F250 is all set up for heavy-duty four-wheeling. No way it can get stuck."

The next day I drove over Suman's narrow trail as far as I could before pulling off onto a clearing so I could walk the rest of the way in. As I prepared to turn off the trail, Dan repeated his warning. To ease his mind, I climbed out of the cab and surveyed the clearing on foot. The leaf-covered ground supported my weight easily. "This will do just fine," I said.

I backed the truck in. It promptly sank to the frame in thick, dark ooze that looked like used engine oil.

"What's this?" I said as I climbed down.

Suman looked on with a bemused grin. He knew I was in deep trouble; the top of each tire was barely visible.

I climbed back behind the wheel. I had pulled the truck out of some of Missouri's worst mud, so I wasn't overly concerned about this little Michigan mudhole.

But try as I might, the mud wouldn't yield its prize. Even in low-range 4WD, the truck was stuck fast.

"What are you going to do now?" Suman asked.

WHEN TROUBLE FINDS YOU

Good question. For starters, hunters and fishermen who routinely venture into rough country should never assume that the vehicle, no matter how well equipped—won't get stuck. At some point, trouble will find even the most careful drivers. That said, a wise approach for the intrepid outdoorsman is to plan for trouble by installing an electric winch. Reduced to essentials, an electric winch is a motorized drum that unspools and spools a length of heavy-duty wire rope. Once the rope has been attached properly to a secure anchor, the winch can draw a 4×4 out of deep mud or off a steep talus slope.

A generation ago these helping hands were bulky accessories that were permanently mounted in massive replacement bumpers. Nowadays you can opt for a detachable quick-mount platform that slides a compact winch into a receiver (front or rear). When the winch isn't needed, the mount and winch slide out for storage in the garage or tool shed.

PICKING THE WINCH

Choosing a winch may seem confusing, but it's really fairly simple. Electric winches are classified by duty ratings, which are based on line pull, gearing system, and motor. Let's look at each, in order.

In engineer-speak, rated line pull (RLP) is the weight the winch can pull perpendicular to the ground with a single layer of wire rope on the drum. (Translation: RLP determines the total weight the winch can handle.) The RLP of most winches runs between 5,000 to 12,000 pounds. That's a broad range. How do you know which RLP is best for your vehicle?

In general, winch manufacturers recommend that you choose a

In general, the rated line pull of a winch determines how much weight it can handle. The RLP of most winches runs between 5,000 to 12,000 pounds. Most manufacturers recommend that your winch be able to pull a load 1.5 times greater than the total weight of the 4×4.
E. Stewart

winch with an RLP that is at least 1.25 to 1.5 times greater than the total weight of your vehicle. That's because the rated line pull of the winch must be high enough to pull the weight of the vehicle while overcoming the very considerable resistance of mud or a steep slope. To ensure the winch has enough gumption, always round up to a higher rating. You've heard the phrase "less is more?" Well, that doesn't apply to winch capacity. In this case, "when in doubt, oversize."

The key to choosing the proper RLP is knowing exactly how much your vehicle weighs when fully loaded. That means curb weight plus the weight of your hunting and fishing gear, a full fuel tank, and the weight of your buddies—none of whom are on low-carb diets. Fully loaded, the truck could easily weigh 2,000 pounds more than curb weight. If you buy on curb weight only, you won't have enough winch.

The best way to get an accurate weight reading is to load the vehicle, round up your buddies, then take it to a sand and gravel pit, grain elevator, building and supply company, county waste disposal site, or moving company. These facilities have large drive-on scales, and for a nominal fee you'll get an accurate read on your truck's total weight.

Now let's consider cable length and diameter. In general, cable diameter increases with the RLP. Typically, you'll find 1/4-inch cable on lighter RLP winches and 3/8-inch cable on heavier-duty models.

Cable length is a little more complicated. Actual line rating will vary depending on how many layers are wound on the drum of the winch. You can expect a 10 percent drop in rating for each layer of wire rope that remains on the drum.

In other words, a 9,000-pound winch reaches full rating with one

Actual line rating in the field will vary depending on how many layers of wire rope are wound on the drum. You can expect a 10 percent drop in line rating for each layer of wire rope that remains on the drum.
E. Stewart

layer of line on the drum, but drops to 5,400 pounds with four layers on the drum. Say you have a 9,000-pound winch with 95 feet of cable. Manufacturers say that the average amount of line pulled out is 40 to 50 feet. That means that the real line rating is closer to 6,200 to 7,300 pounds, which can still handle the hypothetical example above. (Don't work yourself into a lather about this. Manufacturer catalogs explain line rating in easy-to-fathom charts.)

Most manufacturers recommend a minimum of 75 feet of cable. If you do most of your hunting, fishing, and camping in the East, Midwest, and South, where trees are easy to find, 75 feet of cable is usually all you need. But if you four-wheel in high-desert sage flats or the prairie grassland, where trees are few and far between, go with at least 150 feet of cable.

Winch motors are either series wound or permanent magnet. Series-wound motors are more suited to longer duration use; permanent-magnet motors require a lower amperage draw. For high-traction applications with full-size trucks, I'm partial to series-wound motors.

The multiple gears found in a planetary-gear winch mean greater pulling speed; the cylindrical worm and round gear of a worm-gear winch, on the other hand, offer significantly greater gear reduction. In this case, you get brute strength but oh-so-slow operation. In general, outdoorsmen will find the faster-working planetary gears best for their applications.

In addition to selecting the winch, you also need to know about accessories, most of which come with the winch. Generally, the accessory kit includes recovery straps, tree protector strap, clevis (which allows you to connect the wire rope to the tree protector strap), optional remote control system, snatch blocks (also known as pulley blocks), tow hooks, and heavy gloves.

The key to safe winch operation is selecting a stout anchor point. Large trees are a good anchor. Make sure to use a tree protector strap so the tree isn't harmed. Never wrap the wire rope around the tree.
E. Stewart

USING THE WINCH

The key to safe winch operation is selecting a stout anchor point. Choose wisely, as winching can generate extreme mechanical forces; if the anchor breaks free—well, to put it in the vernacular, all hell will break loose. Trees, large boulders, and other vehicles make good anchors. If you choose a tree, make sure that it's alive (dead ones topple easily) and that the roots are deep (under towing stress, shallow roots may cause the tree to uproot). Trust me here; I learned both the hard way.

The two most common setups are the single-line pull and the double-line pull.

To rig for a single-line pull, remove the nylon tree strap protector from the winch accessory package. Position it flat and low against the anchor. Next, run the clevis through both loops of the protector and secure with the pin. Put the clutch in freespool, then pull out the wire rope from the drum. Insert the hook at the end of the wire rope into the clevis. (Never wrap the rope around an anchor and then hook it back onto itself. Doing so creates kinks that can cause the rope to break under a load. Wrapping the wire rope around a tree will also damage the tree.) Lay a blanket or tarp over the wire rope about halfway between the winch and the anchor. This helps direct the rope to the ground if it breaks under load.

Slowly take up the slack, then conduct a final inspection of the rigging before powering up to full load. Have your partner climb into the truck so he can steer the vehicle and apply throttle when needed. With a long remote cord, you can also operate the winch from the cab if necessary.

The double-line pull uses a snatch block (also known as a pulley

The single-line pull is the basic winch setup. Once the wire rope has been attached to the tree protector, place a tarp or old blanket over the rope. This helps direct the rope to the ground if it breaks under load. Slowly take up slack, and then conduct a final inspection of the rigging before powering up to full load.
E. Stewart

block) to run the wire rope out to an anchor and then double it back to the vehicle, where the hook is attached to the frame—not the bumper, winch, or any part of the suspension. This rig gives you a two-to-one mechanical advantage over single-line pulling and is useful when the vehicle is really mired. Keep in mind that the anchor will bear the brunt of this double load, so pick a stout one. Also, doubling the power cuts the winch speed in half.

DOWN TO BUSINESS

The reason I had been so cavalier about getting stuck was that I had taken one big precaution. I had added a Superwinch S9000 to the F250. With a rated line pull of 9,000 pounds, I figured it could handle anything Suman's woods could throw at it. And because I installed the winch on a Superwinch portable winch platform, the unit slipped into the front receiver nearly as easily as if I were sliding in a Class III drawbar.

But I must admit: This black mud was evil-looking stuff. Fortunately, the truck was positioned directly in front of some nearby trees, so I was assured an easy single-line pull, the simplest and most common winch setup.

Once the winch was properly rigged, I handed the remote control to Suman and hopped into the cab. The instant I felt the front tires lurch forward, I applied some throttle and the truck popped free.

Then I walked back to the gaping hole behind the truck. I could see Suman shaking his head; the imprint of the F250's leaf springs were clearly visible in the mud. So was something else—a large, sunken tree trunk. No wonder the truck had been unable to free itself; the mud-clogged rear tires couldn't climb over the slippery trunk. Even if the front tires had been able to gain purchase, the tree trunk effectively blocked any forward motion.

Take that as positive proof that the unexpected can sink you when you drive offroad. But if you prepare for trouble by bringing along a healthy dose of common sense and the proper equipment, you'll make the going a lot smoother.

SAFETY TIPS

An electric winch, like any powerful tool, needs to be treated with respect. Keep in mind the slogan that test pilots commit to memory: *The sky is not inherently unsafe; it is just supremely unforgiving of error.*

Here are some quick do's and don'ts regarding winch operation. Do:

- Wear heavy work gloves (which protect against sharp burrs when handling a wire-rope winch cable).
- Place wheel blocks behind the tires when winching vehicle up an incline.
- Disconnect the remote control when the winch is not in use.
- Periodically inspect the winch mount.
- Keep yourself and others a safe distance from the winch cable. Onlookers should stand as far back as the length of the cable that's been reeled out. You can protect yourself from a snapping cable by opening the hood or standing behind an open door.
- Double-check all connections and anchor points before operating the winch.
- Make sure the cable spools evenly onto the drum when you rewind it.

When re-spooling wire rope, make sure it lies evenly on the spool.
E. Stewart

Don't:
- Allow the winch to overheat. The motor has been designed for intermittent, not continuous use; if it becomes hot to the touch, stop and allow it to cool down.
- Don't stick hands inside the drum of the winch.
- Don't operate any winch that has a frayed wire-rope cable or a damaged hook.
- Don't move the vehicle to take slack out of the cable. Always use the winch to ensure a taut line.

13

Matching the Hitch

Safe towing begins at the rear of your 4×4.

IF YOU'RE IN THE MARKET for a trailer hitch, you'd do well to keep in mind the dry fly trout fisherman. For best results, the dry fly fisherman should match the hatch, picking a fly based on the size, color, and silhouette of the natural insects he sees on the water. Well, the prospective tower should do the same and match the hitch to the tow vehicle. This is important, whether you're ordering a new pickup, installing a hitch on an older vehicle, or simply upgrading present equipment. Mismatched hitches not only deliver poor performance, they are downright dangerous. An overloaded hitch can fail, causing the trailer to separate from the tow vehicle with potentially catastrophic consequences.

Though the majority of hunters and fishermen don't consider hitch installation a do-it-yourself job, the more you know about hitch types and classes, the better the chance of getting what you want. Since hitches are classified by the weight they're designed to haul, matching the hitch starts by establishing the weight of the trailer and the towing capacity of the tow vehicle.

WEIGHTY MATTERS

"When you leaf through the owner's manual, you'll come across several weight-rating terms. There'll all important, but most owners find them confusing," says Joe Hige, marketing director at Draw-Tite. "First, gross vehicle weight rating (GVWR). This is a measure of the total weight capacity of the vehicle, including driver, passengers, cargo,

Matching the hitch starts by determining the weight of the trailer and boat and the towing capacity of the vehicle.

fluids, accessories, and the tongue weight of the trailer. Many truck owners mistakenly believe that the truck's GVWR can be increased through the installation of heavier springs, air bags, and other devices. In truth, these add-ons affect ride quality and the vehicle's ability to maintain level ride height; they do not increase the GVWR. Because this rating is a key to safe towing, never exceed it.

"Second, the gross axle weight rating (GAWR). This tells you the maximum weight each axle can safely carry.

"Finally, there is the gross combined weight rating (GCWR), which takes into account the combined weight of the tow vehicle and trailer, including all passengers, cargo, and fluids contained in both. In simple terms, if the truck weighs out at 7,000 pounds and has a GCWR of 10,000 pounds, the total weight of the trailer cannot exceed 3,000 pounds."

The other weight figures crucial to safe towing are the gross trailer weight (GTW) and tongue weight (TW). The GTW is the weight of the fully loaded trailer. All trailers have a maximum weight rating, which must not be exceeded. Tongue weight is the downward force exerted on the hitch ball by the trailer coupler. In most cases it is about 10 to 15 percent of the GTW. The most accurate way to determine the weight of your trailer is to weigh it at a commercial scale.

With these figures in hand you can now make sure the intended tow vehicle can handle the trailer. Under no circumstances should you exceed the tow vehicle's maximum weight rating.

THE HITCH FOR YOU

Now you're ready to determine the type and class of hitch needed. Despite the multitude of available hitches, the field basically divides into two types: weight-carrying hitches and weight-distributing hitches, subdivided by weight ratings, called classes.

Weight-carrying hitches support the tongue weight of the trailer at the hitch ball and are generally used for lightweight trailers up to 3,500 pounds GTW and 300 pounds TW. Pickups and sport utilities with heavy-duty towing packages can use weight-carrying hitches up to 5,000 pounds GTW and 500 pounds TW. Weight-carrying hitches come in two styles: fixed drawbar/ball mount and removable drawbar/ball mount (also known as a receiver hitch). With a fixed drawbar/ball mount hitch, the ball platform is a permanent member welded to the hitch; with a receiver, the ball platform is removable.

Weight-distributing hitches distribute tongue weight to all vehicle and trailer axles. Heavier trailers can be towed when the tongue weight is distributed in this way. These hitches also keep the tow vehicle's rear from sagging and help improve steering and braking control. The hitches are available only in removable drawbar/ball mount (receiver) styles and can handle as much as 10,000 pounds GTW and 1,000 pounds TW.

Hitch classes are simply weight ratings. Weight-carrying hitches have three classes:

CLASS	GTW (maximum)	TW (maximum)
I	2,000 pounds	200 pounds
II	3,500 pounds	300 pounds
III	3,500–5,000 pounds	350–500 pounds

Class III trailer hitches are available as receivers only. The other two hitch classes offer both receiver and fixed drawbar/ball mount models.

The Class III hitch is the most popular choice for hunters and fishermen. It can handle as much as 5,000 pounds.
E. Stewart

Weight-distributing hitches have two classes:

CLASS	GTW (maximum)	TW (maximum)
III	4,000 pounds	350 pounds
IV	5,000–12,000 pounds	500–1,200 pounds

Generally, the Class I hitch is used to tow very small boats, such as a 12-foot aluminum skiff with a trolling motor and small pop-up camping trailers. These hitches are suitable for only the lightest of towing applications. Many Class I hitches are actually step-bumper hitches. (This type of hitch is simply a ball placed directly into the truck's bumper.) Over the years I've seen too many crumpled step bumpers—which tell me that the hitch and the load are too often mismatched.

The majority of hunters and fishermen opt for a Class III weight-carrying hitch because of its overwhelming versatility and ease of use. But if you tend to tow really heavy loads, move up to a Class IV and invest in a weight-distributing hitch.

CRITICAL LINKS

Three other critical links—the hitch ball, the wiring connector, and safety chains—complete the basic safe towing package. Hitch balls must match the trailer coupler size and the GTW. Hitch balls come in three sizes: $1^7/8$, 2, and $2^5/16$ inches. The most common size is 2 inches. Size matters! Always match the ball to the size of the trailer coupler. If you choose a ball that's too small, sudden disconnection could result.

Trailer wiring systems consist of tail lights, brakes, and a variety of running lights. Four-way plug connectors are the most common and include wires for tail and running lights, turn signals and brake lights, and a ground. Other common connector types include flat, square, round, and five-, six-, and seven-way connectors. Tell the installer the type of connector found on your trailer. (Note: Truck wiring harnesses generally use a four-plug connector. Not so with trailers. Double-check the wiring connector on your trailer—or any trailer you intend to buy—to see if it's compatible with the truck connector. Chances are the plugs won't match; in this case, you'll

Trailer wiring systems consist of tail lights and a variety of running lights. Four-way plug connectors are the most common.
E. Stewart

If the truck and trailer plug connector don't match, an adapter (available from a towing accessory store) will allow you to connect truck and trailer wiring systems.
E. Stewart

need an adapter, which is available at any well-stocked towing accessories store.)

Safety chains help prevent disaster if the tow vehicle and trailer become separated. Criss-cross the chains underneath the trailer tongue to form a cradle. If the trailer comes loose, the tongue will fall onto the cradle, keeping the trailer behind the tow vehicle until you can stop safely. As an added measure of safety, place a bolt or pin through the coupler latch after securing the trailer to the tow vehi-

Safety chains help prevent disaster if the tow vehicle separates from the hitch. Criss-cross the chains underneath the trailer tongue to form a cradle. If the trailer comes loose, the tongue will fall onto the cradle, keeping the trailer behind the tow vehicle until you can safely stop the truck.
E. Stewart

When securing the drawbar/ballmount into the receiver, slip the pin in from the driver's side of the receiver.

cle. This will help keep the coupler from accidentally opening while you're driving. Finally, when securing the drawbar/ball mount into the receiver, slip the pin in from the driver's side of the receiver. Roads are "crowned," which means the surface is slightly higher in the middle; the drop-off to the edge helps the road drain faster. Inserting the pin from the driver's side of the receiver takes advantage of this and will help keep it in place if the safety clip falls off.

ON THE LEVEL

A level-riding trailer is essential to safe towing. When hooked up, you want the trailer tongue to ride parallel to the ground. This allows the trailer to track straight behind the tow vehicle.

To maintain level trailer height, hitch installers use ball mounts and drawbars in a "hitch drop/rise configuration." This is simply a measure of how many inches the hitch ball must drop or rise in order to keep the trailer level. Hitch drop/rise is required because of the height difference between the body of the tow vehicle and the trailer. Generally, a compact four-wheel-drive pickup or sport utility uses a ball mount with a 2-inch drop. Full-size four-wheel-drive pickups and sport utilities generally employ a ball mount drop of 3 inches. But if the truck has been lifted or rides on taller tires, you may require a drop of 6 to 10 inches to keep the trailer level.

"A word of caution here," says Hige. "The deeper the drop or rise, the less weight the ball mount can support. For this reason, the tow rating on a vehicle with a drop or rise of 6 inches or more is only 2,000 pounds. So if you intend to do a lot of heavy-duty towing, don't give your truck a radical lift."

A level-riding trailer is essential to safe towing. Hitch installers will drop or raise the ball mount to maintain level trailer height. Generally, a 4WD truck will use a 2- to 3-inch drop, though vehicles with suspension lifts may require a drop of 4 inches or more.
E. Stewart

If the hitch drop/rise is correct, but the vehicle still isn't level, see if the springs need to be replaced. If not, you may need to install beefier springs or auxiliary air springs. You should also check to make sure you haven't exceed the recommended tongue weight.

Keeping the vehicle level is vital. A truck with its nose in the air is unbalanced; it won't handle properly, and its ability to brake safely will be seriously compromised.

EQUIPMENT CHECK

For best results while towing a boat or trailer, make sure the tow vehicle is equipped to do the job. This means more than the hitch. Towing places severe stress on the vehicle, which is why manufacturers offer special towing packages that include heavy-duty radiators and alternators, heavy-duty shocks and springs, and auxiliary transmission coolers. If you intend to do a lot of towing, make sure your vehicle is equipped with these options.

BACKING UP

The maneuver that probably creates the most stress for inexperienced towers is backing down the launch ramp. Do yourself a favor: Don't try this on a busy weekend.

Backing the trailer down a ramp (or in a service area, for that matter) isn't all that hard, but, like establishing the proper lead in wingshooting, it takes practice. The key fact to bear in mind is that the trailer will always go in the opposite direction of the tow vehicle.

Backing up a trailer is a difficult maneuver for beginners because truck and trailer seem to have minds of their own. Here's a way to make the process easier: Place your hand at the bottom of the steering wheel. When you move your hand to the right, the trailer moves to the left; when you move your hand to the left, the trailer will move to the right. Practice makes perfect.
E. Stewart

This causes a great deal of confusion and is one of the main reasons you see guys jockeying up and down the ramp with a trailer that seems to have a mind of its own.

Here's how to handle the situation. First, find a big empty parking lot. This way you can spend the time necessary to gain control over the maneuver without worrying about a long line of irate fishermen behind you. Then, put your left hand on the bottom of the steering wheel. When you move your hand to the right (which turns the front wheels of the truck to the left), the trailer will move to the right. When you move your hand to the left (which turns the front wheels of the truck to the right), the trailer will move to the left. It takes a little getting used to, but it works.

The other key is to move slowly. Most beginners back up too fast, which only makes the problem worse. And here's another tip to keep in mind when you are on the ramp. If the trailer starts to move in the wrong direction, stop, pull forward until the trailer is straight, and begin again. Trying to correct a wayward trailer will only make matters worse.

PRO TOWING TIPS

Sam Anderson is a young touring pro on the walleye circuit. Between his fishing and promotion work, he drives through 17 states a year, mainly the northern half of the country. He tows in all kinds of weather and terrain, and his tips are worth a listen.

- "First, do a walk-around inspection of the truck and trailer. Make sure everything is stowed properly on the boat. You'd be amazed how many fishing rods are lost each year because someone forgets to secure them properly with a tie-down or put them in a rod locker."
- "One of the accessories I regularly inspect—and almost never see anyone even look at—is windshield wipers. This is critical. Try driving 5 or 6 hours in bad weather with worn-out wipers. It's bad enough during the day; at night, when you're tired, forget it. You're an accident waiting to happen."
- "Check the air pressure on the vehicle and trailer tires. A lot of people check the tires on their truck but forget the trailer. Make sure that the tire pressure is in the recommended range because of the extra weight you're hauling. Properly inflated tires will also help the tow vehicle deliver maximum fuel economy, and when you tow, every gallon counts."
- "Check the wiring harness regularly for signs of corrosion that could cause the trailer running lights and brake lights to fail. Northern drivers take note: Road salt is a certified killer of electrical connections."
- "Check the trailer wheel hubs regularly. Most people check the hubs once a year. I do it every time I stop for fuel. Why? Because of the heat that towing generates. You want to make sure the hubs still have adequate grease, and it's a whole lot better to stop at a service station and get it fixed than have the hubs lock up in the middle of nowhere. And let me tell you, you don't want to deal with a hub failure at highway speed; it's nasty business. I know some guys who won't even go on the road without spare bearings packed in grease and stored in sealed plastic bags in case of emergencies."

CHAPTER 14

Getting Out There . . . and Back

Easy does it.

FROM THE TOP of the hill, I could see for miles. The rugged mountain terrain was dotted with ponderosa pine and manzanita, and the pungent smell of sage was in the air. "Keep your eyes open," my host said. "We've got mule deer, bears, bobcats, turkeys, mountain lions, and coyotes up here."

"Up here" was California's San Bernardino National Forest, where at 8,500 feet I was getting a lesson in 4×4 driving tactics from Gary Steffens, a reserve deputy sheriff for the San Bernardino County Sheriff's Department. For more than 25 years Steffens and his search-and-rescue team have been called upon to find hunters and fishermen who have gotten stranded in this huge expanse of desert and alpine forest. As a lifelong outdoorsman, Steffens knows all about the lure of remote hunting and fishing locations; as a trained offroad driving and survival expert, he is also well acquainted with what can go wrong when you venture deep into the wilderness. So pay attention; his tips have been honed by years of experience. They'll help you get out there . . . and back.

EASY DOES IT

Many drivers believe that the faster the vehicle goes through a rough section, the better. Not so. If the vehicle builds up too much speed when it hits a deep hole or rock, the resulting loss of control can

Wheel spin (the result of a heavy foot on the throttle) usually means that you're not in control of the situation. Slow down. You want enough momentum to carry you through the sand or mud, but not so much that you can't completely control the vehicle.

send the 4×4 bouncing off the trail or wedge the nose or rear tight into a rut. Either way, it's bad news.

Steffens prefers momentum to speed. "Momentum implies control—because the vehicle moves just fast enough to overcome an obstacle while remaining in the driver's complete control. To me, momentum also means staying off the brake as much as possible," he says.

"Wheel spin [the result of a heavy foot on the throttle] usually means that you're not in control of the situation," he says. "So slow down. Remember, you want enough momentum to carry you through the sand or over the boulders, but not enough so you can't control the vehicle. *Easy does it.*"

Steffens also advises that you use the engine braking created by low-range four-wheel-drive rather than the brakes to help slow the vehicle during a steep descent. This way you can avoid locking the brakes—which leads to a loss of steering and, ultimately, trouble.

STAY ON TOP

When faced with a deeply rutted trail, Steffens advises, "Ride the ridges." Ruts can be caused naturally—by erosion—or deliberately—

When faced with a deeply rutted trail, riding the ridges can
help keep the vehicle above ruts
that can trap it.
E. Stewart

by drivers who run the trails after wet weather. Either way, a trail
that's been chewed up will be pockmarked with deep gullies, any
one of which can snag a 4×4. Most commonly, you'll high-center the
vehicle, but sometimes the gully will trap the nose or the rear
instead.

"If you can stay on top of the ridges, you'll ride above the ruts,"
Steffens says. This is demanding driving; if the vehicle slips off the
ridge and into the rut, chances are you'll be there awhile.

BE PREPARED

To borrow a phrase from the Boy Scouts, be prepared. "In really
rugged terrain, the 4×4 should have a winch, Hi-Lift Jack [a special

Be prepared. This bird hunter built
storage drawers to hold a wide
assortment of emergency gear in
case he gets stranded in the
backcountry.

and highly versatile offroad tool, see the Appendix], shovel, fire extinguisher, pry bar, and tire chains. Most people think of tire chains only for snow, but I consider them to be essential all-weather extra-traction equipment. I also recommend plenty of drinking water—in winter as well as summer—and a couple of rolls of duct tape. You can never have enough duct tape."

UP AROUND THE BEND

When still-hunting for deer, the experienced hunter takes a step or two, then pauses to look for sign. Only after thoroughly inspecting the cover around him does he then proceed—slowly—to take another step or two.

Now put that guy behind the wheel of a 4×4, and chances are he simply charges up the trail. He has no idea what's around the bend, or how deep that water crossing really is.

"Trails aren't static," Steffens says. "Even if it's one you drive every year, weather conditions may have changed the surface since your last trip. The stream may be running higher and the ruts may be deeper. A rock slide may block the way. The last thing you want to do is back the vehicle down a trail. That would be exceedingly unpleasant. I'd rather be safe than sorry. That's why I tell people to get out and walk over any portion of a trail that looks as if it might be a problem. It may look fine from the bottom, but halfway up you may find that the ruts are too deep. The only way to know for sure is to get out of the vehicle and scout the trail."

If you don't know what's up ahead, get out and walk. Trails aren't static; they change from year to year, and you need to know exactly what lies ahead.
E. Stewart

Steffens and I took 2 hours to cover 6 miles of rugged, rut-covered trail and, as he noted, "We're not even on the tough trail!" In essence, his experience boils down to a simple phrase all offroad sportsmen should commit to memory: Be safe rather than sorry.

OFFROAD SURVIVAL TIPS

Gary Steffens has been on more than 400 search-and-rescue operations in blistering heat as well as in the deep cold and snow of winter. Here are four of his rules for backcountry survival.

1. Check weather conditions. "In some areas, especially in the mountains, the weather may be sunny and warm at the beginning of the day and be cold and snowy by nightfall. Always check with the weather service before you head out. You want to know what they expect the weather to do for the next 24 hours or more. Wind, wet, and cold lead to hypothermia, and you can find these conditions in late spring and early fall as well as winter. Always bring extra blankets, clothing, food, and water."

2. Tell somebody where you're going. "We've had numerous occasions where someone just took off. They haven't told anyone where they're going or what time they expect to return. This is tough for our search-and-rescue team because we patrol several hundred square miles of national forest.

   "The best way to help someone find you is to draw a copy of your specific route on another map and leave that copy behind.

   "The other problem we have is that sometimes people change their plans en route. When they don't return, we go to where they said they would be, but we don't find them. At that point we're looking for a needle in a haystack. If you change your plans, let the people at home know the new destination. And don't depend on a cell phone. Out here, they often don't work."

3. Traveling alone. "Don't. Offroaders should always travel in pairs. That way they'll have another vehicle to assist in an emergency."

4. Stay put. "If you think you're lost, stay put. Find shelter while it's still daylight. Don't panic. Common sense will get you through most situations."

Experienced offroaders don't travel alone; they know unexpected emergencies can crop up at any moment. Though this field looked dry, a few moments after the photo was taken the driver sank up to the axles in mud. He had to be towed out.

OFFROAD ODDS AND ENDS

Terrain is a constantly changing challenge. While offroad you will drive over many different surfaces—hard-packed dirt, gravel, rocks, sand, mud, snow, and ice. Each affects the steering, acceleration, and braking in different ways. Depending on just what kind of surface you're on, you may encounter slipping, sliding, wheel spin, poor traction, and longer braking distances. You will also encounter obstacles such as rocks, stumps, and logs.

The best advice I ever got about dealing with trail obstacles came from an offroad driver who said, "The best way to approach obstacles is to think of a hurdler. Ever notice that his head stays level as he jumps each hurdle? That's because he's letting his legs do all the work. Well, when you encounter a log, stump, or rock, let the vehicle's suspension and tires do the work."

Small rocks can be straddled. Generally, it's best to position the vehicle so the rock passes under the driver's side. That's because the front differential—usually the lowest hanging component—is often (but not always) located to the right. (Check the position of the differentials in your vehicle before you go offroad.) Larger rocks can be driven over. Ease the tire over each obstacle.

If you drive carefully, feathering both the brake and the accelerator so you ease each wheel over an obstacle, you'll in essence be keeping your head level. Doing so not only makes the ride considerably more comfortable, but it also helps keep the wheels on the ground, which helps maintain control.

Don't develop tunnel vision, where you focus only on what is immediately in front of you. Take the time to see what's farther down the trail, as well as what's on either side. In addition, most drivers

Small rocks can be straddled. Just make sure that no low-hanging vehicle components will hit the obstacle.
E. Stewart

Larger rocks can be driven over. In this case, it's best to have a partner spot for you, using hand signals to tell you how to inch over the rock or stump.
E. Stewart

tend to look more to the left than to the right and to steer to the right to avoid overhanging objects. (This trait can make drivers so intent on clearing the left side of the truck that they run the right side into a tree.)

The customary advice to picking the proper gear for hill climbing is to always shift into the lowest gear available in order to get the best traction. Basically, that's sound advice, but a better approach is to pick the highest gear capable of ensuring steady progress. On some hills, first gear provides too much power, and the result is dirt-throwing wheel spin and a consequent loss of traction.

Throughout the ascent, keep in mind that hill climbing is not a commando exercise to see who is king of the mountain; it's a slow, steady process. In fact, every time the wheels leave the ground you lose some control of the vehicle.

CHAPTER 15

The Happy Truck Camper

Comfort rules.

W
HEN I WAS YOUNGER and tougher (in other words, broke and ignorant) I enjoyed roughing it when I hunted and fished with my friends. Our camps were bare-bones affairs, and I still remember my old $2 chicken-feather surplus Army sleeping bag that had no warming properties whatsoever and a canvas tent (also surplus) that leaked like a sieve in a light mist. We preferred the romance of the open fire (we didn't have a gas stove), so cooking meant impaling channel cats on green sticks and then squatting and coughing over a smoky fire.

Later there was a short-lived minimalist stage where I slept out in the open wrapped in a cheap plastic tarp. On clear nights I marveled at the white smear in the sky we know as the Milky Way; on cloudy nights I learned to fear the first faint drops of rain.

I still have buddies who enjoy backpacking or striking off to a spike camp, and they willingly sacrifice certain creature comforts because of a lack of adequate carrying capacity. Not me. Nowadays I camp out of the back of a big truck. Why? Because my rig lets me indulge myself. I take what I want and treat myself to all the luxuries of a newfound five-star hotel.

By big, I mean full-size pickups and sport utilities, vehicles with the necessary room to store all your gear.

You'd be amazed at how even a half-truckload of the right items can move the pleasure needle into the *ahh-yes!* zone. Oversize captain's chairs, a camp kitchen, thick airbeds, cots, a folding table, and coolers full of your favorite eats and drinks are some of the extras that are worth their weight (and space) in gold.

The fellow who taught me the virtues of *ahh-yes* camping is Jim Reid, director of public relations for The Coleman Company. I first spoke with him about truck camping after a disastrous three-day outing in which I had elected to sleep in the bed of the pickup because the tent could not accommodate three adults, one of whom snored loud enough to wake the dead. At the time Jim and I were comfortably ensconced in his camp after a long, hard day of quail hunting along the Kansas-Oklahoma border. He had just made the appetizer— fresh quail soup—and was preparing the main meal—grilled Kansas City strip steaks—as we enjoyed a libation. I noticed that for the first time in camp I was warm, comfortable, and completely relaxed.

"Yeah," Jim said. "Basically, the happy camper is the one who sleeps well and eats well. Add convenience and comfort while loafing in camp, a righteous cocktail hour, and a big campfire, and you have all the ingredients for a world-class camp."

"So, how can you make sure you get a comfortable camp?" I asked.

GIMME SHELTER

"First step," Reid told me, "is a fundamental human need: shelter. Take a big tent and make no apologies. Two guys can set up today's spacious shelters in under 10 minutes. You'll have plenty of headroom to stand when dressing and you can bunk at the far ends of a 15- to 17-foot-long tent to minimize disturbing one another while sleeping. You'll also have room to store gear bags and all the assorted hunting, fishing, and camping stuff we all insist on taking. A big tent is especially welcome on those rainy days or evenings when waiting out a storm. Eat inside in dry comfort. Put on a new reel or organize that cluttered tackle box. Take a nap. You make the call."

Though there are many tents on the market today, the traditional cabin tent is nearly extinct (except for certain applications such as elk camp). What you'll find, instead, is an array of hybrids that borrow design and function features from tents, geodomes, and cantilevers, then marry them to cabins.

A comfortable camp makes the experience that more enjoyable and relaxing. Don't skimp on the size of the tent.
E. Stewart

"The Coleman Weathermaster is a prime example," Reid says. "The 17×9-foot model features a rainfly for double-layer protection from cloudbursts. It's designed to stand up to winds over 40 mph and manages water runoff without leakage. Like most contemporary tents, it's constructed of coated nylon for strength and foul-weather performance, yet it's relatively light in weight. A color-coded, shock-corded pole system ensures quick, foolproof setup—all at a price under $200. Large windows and a door offer good ventilation options on warm nights, making the Weathermaster a viable three-season tent."

Another option is a large dome tent, a good choice for a one-nighter or when you want to go a little lighter and don't mind surrendering some elbow room. Domes with full rainflies are very weatherworthy. Some models are tall enough to stand up in, at least in the center, and they come in a wide variety of sizes, color, and price tags. No matter what kind of tent you decide on, buy a good one. Cheap tents, as I learned the hard way a long time ago, aren't worth the money.

BIG SLEEP

"Sleeping well should be simple," Reid says. "Select the right sleeping bag, add a comfortable mattress system, your favorite pillow, and you should sleep soundly. The right bag is one that meets the prevailing temperature conditions, is an appropriate size, and features a liner and cover that match your individual preference.

"Too many people think all sleeping bags are created equal. Not so. There are oversized bags to fit big folks or to give the average-sized adult extra room."

Temperature ratings are critical to picking the right bag, especially in cooler weather. If you tend to chill easily at home, take that into consideration. If you expect the nighttime temperature to be in the 30s and 40s, say, don't be afraid to take a bag rated for 15° F. You might even opt for a bag rated for 0° F. You can always vent the bag with two-way zippers or otherwise get some fresh air in to moderate the temperature.

If the temperature becomes unseasonably warm, carry along a light blanket; then peel back the top of the bag and cover your upper torso with the blanket. For really cold weather, nothing beats a mummy bag for warming efficiency.

"Many people like the cozy feel of a flannel liner," Reid says. "Others want nylon inside and out. The choice is yours. Temperature ratings run from –25° F (or cooler) to 50° F. If you're a four-season camper, you can't expect one bag to do it all."

Reid was an early advocate of good camp airbeds. "They're a godsend for backs, young and old," he says. "Especially old. Our QuickBed is 6 inches thick and provides excellent support and comfort. For added convenience, it can be inflated in less than 3 minutes using our innovative battery-powered QuickPump inflator. This way you won't have to drag the bed out to the truck's 12-volt inflator."

The airbed works fine on the tent floor, but for added comfort put the airbed on an oversize, sturdy cot. That gets you off the ground, making it easy to get into and out of the rack. The cot also provides a handy storage space for boots, duffle bags, and the like.

GOOD EATS

A well-appointed camp galley makes a world of difference to outdoorsmen who cherish harvest-style breakfasts, brunches, and food-fest dinners. Even in the best "improved" campgrounds, you'll discover a hard truth: A steel fire ring and a listing picnic table make for poor meal preparation, unless Spam, Saltines, and Vienna sausages are your fare *du jour.*

Proper food preparation is essential to a great camp. The Coleman Camp Kitchen (shown in carrying case) holds everything needed to produce great camp fare, plus it folds up for easy storage and transport.
E. Stewart

Years ago I used to make an annual fishing/camping trip with old friends on Virginia's Shenandoah River. Though our self-elected camp cook had obvious talent, somehow grit always found its way into every meal, prompting one member of our group to proclaim late one night, "Why is it that every time you cook I need to get my teeth re-enameled?" Amid hoots of laughter, the essential truth had been revealed: Our camp lacked an adequate food preparation area.

Reid never travels without a Coleman Camp Kitchen. "Picture a 35-pound slender suitcase that opens up into 6 feet of cooking space," he says. "There's a long wide shelf for the camp stove. Another large counterspace for slicing and dicing. A sink. Racks for spices, condiments, matches, soap, and such. It's even got hooks for utensils, hotpads, and a can opener as well as a paper towel rack."

Though Reid has used a single-burner backpacking stove, he prefers something a bit more substantial. "The three-burner camp stove is my choice because it's so convenient. At breakfast, one burner can be brewing that all-important first pot of coffee while the other two are free to heat a griddle or two big skillets. Our Guide Series propane stove is set up to run from a bulk propane tank, which means you won't have to worry about running out of fuel while feeding your hungry crew. The 15,000 BTUs of the left-most burner will let you brew the fastest coffee in the West, which is important for those early wakeup calls at deer camp. The other two burners put out 10,000 BTUs."

CAMP BOX

Most veteran campers develop a camp box that holds pots, pans, and essential utensils and accessories. The idea is simple: The box is always loaded and ready to travel. A few years ago I fished for rainbow trout in the high desert sagebrush country of eastern Oregon with Dave Hughes and Ted Leeson. We camped three nights, moving from river to river in a Jeep Cherokee. Dave's homemade box made cooking good meals a snap. He built it out of scrap wood "after experiencing one too many trips where some essential cooking utensil—typically the cast-iron skillet—had been left behind."

Your camp box can be as plain or fancy as you like. Hughes built his with swing-away doors and shelves that securely held condiments, utensils, and paper towels. I've seen others that are no more than waterproof plastic boxes, which help keep everything nice and dry.

"The same box, or another, can hold a saw and hand ax, fire-starter sticks, clothesline, rope, twine, duct tape, patch kits, trash bags, camp soap, first-aid kit, knife-sharpening kit, and more," says Reid. "The point is that you need a system that allows you to always have this stuff on hand when you camp. I've also found a printed checklist to be invaluable. Consider it a working document that can be customized over the seasons and altered to suit each trip as necessary."

TABLES AND CHAIRS

"Another item I never leave home without is a lightweight folding table. There's never enough table room at a campsite and many primitive sites lack even a rudimentary picnic table. In addition to helping to cook and serve food, the table can be used for other activities such as cleaning guns or reels, sharpening knives, tying flies, or patching waders."

One of my pet peeves as I age is getting into camp and then having to spend my time sitting in the dirt or perched on a cooler or log. Doing so has a certain romance, I suppose; so does using a saddle for a pillow. But it's not the most relaxing way to go, and as Reid is so

Master of the Comfortable Camp, Jim Reid, director of public relations at The Coleman Company, drives his Suburban into a backcountry camp. He says, "The happy camper is the one who sleeps well and eats well."

fond of saying, "Remember, the primary mission of the trip is to relax, enjoy yourself, and recharge your spiritual batteries. You can't do that if you spend all your time squatting on a log."

Good point. His solution? A comfortable camp chair. They're lightweight and take up about the same room as a standard folding lawn chair. "Our chairs are wide and very stable, with a padded back and arm rests. We also have a rocking-chair model that is just right for observing a sunset or overseeing the lighting of the evening campfire."

COMFORT AND CONVENIENCE

According to Jim Reid, a few more items will add immeasurably to the comfort and convenience of any camp:

- Battery-powered lanterns and flashlights are a must; the more the better. The Coleman Lantern is a fixture in camps nationwide, but there's a new wrinkle—their Remote Control Lantern can be clicked on and off from up to 50 feet away using a keyless-entry-sized device. The light also features a nightlight.
- A catalytic heater can really take the chill off spring or fall mornings and/or evenings. A gas or charcoal grill is most camp chefs' pick for searing steaks, chops, burgers, veggies, and fresh-caught fish.
- High stands, which collapse into very small packages, are handy in camp to get large water jugs or coolers up off the ground and at a useful countertop height.
- A couple of strong polytarps to throw over firewood, tables, and chairs, or to fashion a windbreak or dining fly can save the day.

THE DOWNSIZED CAMPER

Field & Stream Contributing Editor John Merwin is a camper who also knows the value of a comfortable setup. And though he currently hunts and fishes out of a Ford F150, he spent many years using compact pickups. Given that one of his favorite camps is an island on a small lake in New York's Adirondack Mountains, Merwin has learned how to compress his camp into the available space of a canoe.

His camp may be a bit more Spartan than Reid's, but it is still extremely comfortable, as I learned one weekend a couple of years ago. The key for two campers is two canoes, which allow each camper to paddle and fish at his own pace. Into these we put two tents (which we pitched 20 feet apart; John and I are snorers of epic proportions), assorted fishing gear, gas stove, sleeping bags, a big cooler and his camp box, which contained cooking utensils and a well-used blue enamel coffee pot. A single, standard 16-foot canoe will also work for two campers, of course, but in that case you'll be carrying even less gear and will also be fishing the same water at the same time.

"The key to this kind of camping," Merwin told me, "is packing the cooler properly. Here's what you do: Take two 1-gallon plastic milk jugs. Fill one with water, the other with tea. Freeze both. They'll help keep the ice chest cool while they melt. By doing this I don't need to carry another jug of water, or extra ice. To make coffee, I draw water from the lake and when the coffee's done, boil it an extra 10 minutes to kill any organisms or parasites."

Also in the cooler was a plastic food storage box filled with frozen stew. This was the second night's meal, and as it slowly defrosted, it kept other perishables (butter, milk) cold. The first night's meal featured thick steaks, which we grilled over a camp fire. Lunch the next day consisted of fresh-caught rainbow trout rolled in cornmeal.

Merwin also had plenty of light for his camp: a traditional Coleman gas lantern augmented by several small flashlights. His words of wisdom here: "Load up on extra batteries. They don't take up much room."

So even if you use a compact pickup or sport utility, you can still have a good camp. The challenge is utilizing every square inch of storage space. I watched Merwin unpack and pack his truck, and every item—from cooler to canoe, spatula to paddle—had its place.

The Secret to Long Life

The "smart drink" for your 4×4.

THE SECRET TO LONG LIFE is contained in one of the earth's most valuable compounds. No, it's not a magic elixir, it's oil, and the long life it ensures is that of your 4×4s.

Texas-based outfitter Rick Hodges believes in the power of oil. He uses a weathered Ford F350 crew cab to ferry quail and dove hunters from field to field. When I hunted with him a couple of years ago he had logged 225,000 miles on his 6.9-liter diesel, all without a rebuild or major repair. The secret to the engine's long life? Frequent oil and filter changes.

"I change my oil and filter religiously every 3,000 miles," Hodges says. "Out here, my truck has to deal with dust, mud, and water, and I use it to haul feed, trailers, and clients. I'm often in high-rev low-speed situations, like in mud and water, and grinding along in low gear can take a heavy toll on any engine."

Clyde Pritchard, a Nebraska-based hunter, is also a believer. With more than a half-century of experience under his belt, he's seen plenty of 4×4s come and go. Recently, he told me how he was able to put 180,000 miles on an old Jeep Wagoneer. "I hunted all over the Black Hills for deer and pheasants and in Wyoming for antelope, and towed a lot of trailers with it," he said. "The truck did everything I ever asked it to do. The one thing I always did for it was feed it good oil. Because of all that dirt and dust I often changed the oil between 1,500 and 2,000 miles, and I always changed the filter with each oil change.

"I treat my new GMC pickup the same way, and I taught my sons to do the same. But, they've got a friend who has already gone through a couple of engines. He's not stupid; he just doesn't pay attention. Mainly, though, he doesn't change the oil."

Our last testimonial comes from a service technician who specializes in 4×4s. He says, "I've got 136,000 miles on my Suburban. The other day a neighbor dropped by, and when he noted the ding in the front quarter panel and a couple of other rough spots, he told me, 'Your truck is on borrowed time. It's going to rust out!' I told him I would be driving mine when he was three or four cars down the road because he didn't regularly change the oil like I do."

CHANGE YOUR OIL

As you may have figured out by now, changing engine oil regularly is vital to your engine's health and longevity. Yet, it's a detail many truck owners neglect. In fact, a recent survey conducted by the American Automobile Association discovered that nearly one-third of the target vehicles were in need of an oil change. Even more disturbing, the oil level in many of these vehicles was 1 quart low. Given the high cost of engine rebuilds, as well as the prohibitive price of a new truck, this is a senseless waste of money.

Why isn't the oil changed more often? There are a number of reasons, ranging from ignorance to indolence.

Some owners believe their new truck is practically maintenance-free. This is probably the result of improved mechanical reliability and the elimination of some service procedures (periodic lubrication, for one). Unfortunately, as a result, some owners have concluded they can go 10,000 miles between oil changes. That just isn't so.

Frequent oil changes can help your 4×4 live a long time. See the owner's manual for the "severe" service schedule you require.

Although service intervals are much longer than in the past, that mainly applies to cars. Four-wheel-drive owners need to service their vehicles much more frequently.

To find the proper service interval, consult the two maintenance schedules found in the owner's manual. One schedule is for normal operation; the other is for so-called "severe" service. Outdoorsmen need to follow the latter in almost all cases. This schedule is designed for anyone who operates a vehicle in dusty, rough, muddy, or salt-spread roads; who goes on short trips (less than 5 miles) repeatedly; who lives where outside temperatures remain below freezing for long periods of time; who engages in extensive idling and/or low-speed driving; or who tows a trailer or uses a camper or roof carrier.

When you compare the two schedules, you'll note that the severe service schedule generally requires oil changes to be made at nearly twice the rate of the normal service schedule. That's because the kinds of driving outlined above can wear out the oil faster and introduce more contaminates (such as dirt and grit) into the system at a higher rate. Think of it this way: If you shoot your rifle more often, you have to clean it more often.

Failure to follow the schedule can void the warranty—and don't think you can fool a qualified technician. They know that most owners change the oil infrequently, and a quick glance at the engine can tell them whether you've done your job or not.

"The big problem is that many people think they're doing regular oil changes even when they're not," a service technician told me. "I've had guys come in with a bad engine and claim they change the oil every three months, but one look tells me they haven't changed it all year. Many people simply have no idea when the oil was last changed."

Despite the manufacturer's recommendation, many owners feel a once-a-year oil change is good enough. Those in this group complain about the cost (as well as the inconvenience) of oil changes. If you think more frequent oil changes cost too much, consider this: I can change my truck's oil four times a year for about $100. Compare that to the cost of a rebuilt engine, and tell me who's wasting money.

Another false economy involves replacing the oil filter every other oil change or buying bargain-basement filters. This kind of penny-pinching is short-sighted and costly in the long run.

Aftermarket additives may be another reason some owners hold off on oil changes. As one mechanic told me, "You spend $19.95 for an additive, don't tell me the guy's gonna dump it out after only three months. I'm not against additives, but they can't take the place of regular oil and filter changes."

Another common misconception involves vehicles that are used for short trips. Just because you don't put a lot of miles on your 4×4 is no reason not to change the oil frequently. In fact, short trips are worse on oil than long ones. The oil doesn't warm up enough to boil off hydrocarbons and other contaminants. And if these don't boil off, they'll eventually wear out the cylinder walls.

Under the right circumstances, many 4×4s are capable of very long lives, whether measured by the mile or the year. You feed your dog and take it to the vet, don't you? You do it because he's your hunting partner, right? Well, so is your truck. Keep it in good running order, and it will there for the long run.

How Oil Works

Reduced to essentials, engine oil is designed to perform two jobs: 1. lubricate (that is, reduce the friction between the engine's moving parts, such as the crankshaft, bearings, pushrods, and piston rings); and 2. cool (remove the heat created by friction and combustion). Though most folks believe that the primary mission of oil is lubrication, oil company technicians will tell you that cooling is really far more important.

The reason for this is simple: The coolant and radiator can remove only part of the heat created in the modern engine. The vehicle really depends on circulating oil to remove heat from such key components as piston rings, rod and main bearings, timing chain and gears, cylinder walls, and cylinder heads. And here is where penny-pinching on oil filters can hurt you big time: A cheap filter clogs more easily, and a clogged oil filter can hinder oil circulation to the point where cooling ability is so compromised that major mechanical failure—such as burned-out pistons and failed bearings—will result.

All right. Now you know why oil is so important. Next question: what kind of oil should you buy?

Look for the "doughnut" and the "starburst" on the side of every container of quality engine oil. The starburst is the International

When buying oil, look for the "starburst" on the label. It's a certification mark that ensures the oil's quality.
E. Stewart

The other sign of good oil is the "dough-nut," which contains the service rating of the oil.
E. Stewart

Lubricant Standardization and Approval Committee's (ILSAC) certifi-cation mark. It means the product has not only met the service rat-ings created by the American Petroleum Institute (API) but also met additional fuel economy requirements.

The doughnut contains the API Service Rating (the oil indus-try's "bottled-in-bond" equivalent). This is a rating system developed by the API that defines the operational standards that the oil was designed to meet. In essence, it is a measure of the quality of the additives in the oil. Gasoline engine oil is designated SE, SF, SG, or SH (the most current); diesel engine oil is designated CC, CD, CD-II, CE, or CF-4. Don't worry too much about the designations. All you need to do is check your truck's owner's manual. It will tell you which to use.

You can always step up a grade. For instance, if you own an older truck that carries the SF designation, no harm will come if you use SF, SG, or SH oil. However, never go the other way. The performance of newer trucks that require the use of SH oil will suffer if you add SF or SG oil. You will probably void the warranty as well.

ADDITIVES

Additives are supplements designed to extend the life of the oil and enhance its operating qualities. Major additives include:

1. Detergents. Remove grit and other contaminates from operating parts.
2. Foam Inhibitors. Limit the formation of bubbles (foam) created by rotation of the crankshaft and rods, which helps the oil pump work at maximum efficiency.
3. Oxidation Inhibitors. High engine temperatures can create acids that attack metal surfaces. These additives help the oil resist thickening and sludge formation.
4. Friction Modifiers. Reduce friction losses, which help improve fuel economy and power.
5. Anti-Wear Compounds. Help protect components under heavy load (such as the crankshaft rod and main bearings) from premature failure.
6. Corrosion Inhibitors. Reduce rust and wear damage created by acids and moisture.
7. Pour Point Depressants. Improve the ability of oil to flow at very low temperatures. (Used in so-called "winter oils.")
8. Viscosity Index Improver. Helps stabilize the oil's flow capabilities by assisting the oil's natural tendency to fight changes of viscosity with temperature change.

VISCOSITY

Viscosity is an often-misunderstood term. It is commonly referred to as the "weight" of an oil, but weight is not a factor in how well an oil performs. By definition, viscosity is "the resistance to flow exhibited by a liquid." The Society of Automotive Engineers (SAE) uses a numbering system to represent an oil's viscosity at a specific temperature. The higher the number (30, 40), the more resistant (thicker) it is to flow. The lower the number (5, 10), the easier (thinner) it flows.

What does that mean to you?

Engine oils are required to work under extremely demanding conditions. For example, oil must flow easily at very cold temperatures in order to help cool and lubricate the engine. Consider the ice

If you live in an area with bone-numbing cold winters, you should use 5W-30 oil.

fisherman in Minnesota who tries to start the engine when the temperature is −10° F. But the oil must also supply proper lubrication at very high temperatures. In this case, think of an Arizona angler towing his bass boat to Lake Havasu when the desert temperature tops 100° F.

Back when single-viscosity oils were the only choice on the market, some truck owners had to use a high-viscosity oil in summer and then switch to a low-viscosity oil in winter to ensure proper engine oil operation. Fortunately, modern oils are multi-viscosity, which means they are formulated to meet the challenging conditions of winter and summer. Such oils will carry a split viscosity designation such as SAE 5W-30, 10W-40, or 10W-50. (Note: the "W" in such designations does not refer to "weight." It means the oil is rated for winter.)

If you live in an area where summer temperatures are moderate, but winter is foot-numbing cold, go with a 5W-30 oil. If you live in a

If you live in an area where you must endure long periods of very hot weather, invest in 20W-50 oil.

more temperate climate, you can opt for a 10W-30 or 10W-40 oil. The former is best where winters are cold but not bitingly so and where summer sees a few 100° F days; the latter is the choice if you experience mild winters but endure long periods of hot weather— and if you regularly tow a trailer or haul heavy loads. If you live in the desert where temperatures exceed 100° F for weeks at a time, go with 20W-50.

VOLATILITY

Although volatility is related to viscosity, it is even less understood. By definition, volatility is "the characteristic of liquids to become a vapor when heat is applied." The problem is that low-viscosity oils, which are often recommended by vehicle manufacturers because they help the vehicles achieve federal fuel economy standards, tend to evaporate more easily than high-viscosity oils. Owners who use low-viscosity oils often report excessive oil consumption, but the problem is actually evaporation. If you have experienced this problem, look for an oil that has been specially formulated to resist evaporation.

THE SYNTHETIC ALTERNATIVE

Synthetic oils were first developed during World War II and came under a spotlight during the energy crises of the 1970s. When compared to a conventional petroleum-based product, synthetic oil offers improved low temperature operation and better lubrication in high-temperature situations. Synthetics use the same viscosity and service category ratings as regular oil. In addition, some experts believe synthetics perform better in severe-duty situations. But, and it's a big but, synthetic oil costs $2 to $3 more per bottle than regular oil.

THE TALE OF THE STICK

The lowly dipstick remains a great diagnostic tool—if you know what it's telling you. After you check the level of the oil, look closely at the color. Though oil discolors over time, it should not look like tar. If it does, and especially if it smells "burned," it's time for new oil.

The lowly dipstick is a great diagnostic tool. If the oil looks like tar and smells "burned," it's time for a change.
E. Stewart

COOL IT!

Heat is the unavoidable byproduct of power generation, and hard-working trucks need all the cooling capacity they can get. That's why it's important to understand that your truck depends on three separate fluids to dissipate heat: engine oil, automatic transmission fluid (ATF), and antifreeze/coolant. If any one of these systems underperforms, the whole system will suffer. We've just discussed the role of engine oil above; for a thorough discussion of ATF, see Chapter 8. As for coolant, it's best to buy a high-quality brand that resists the buildup of rust and scale in the water jackets of the engine block and heads as well as the radiator. Check the condition of the coolant at regular intervals with an inexpensive coolant system checker, available at any auto parts store.

A mixture of 50 percent water–50 percent antifreeze is a good compromise that will cover most situations. A fresh 50–50 solution will deliver boil-over protection to 265° F and freeze-up protection down to –35° F. If you live in an area that experiences severe winters, you might want to use a 35 percent water–65 percent antifreeze solution, which will provide protection down to –67° F.

A Tale of Two Trucks

*Building the "perfect" hunting
and fishing machines.*

PART 1: THE "ULTIMATE" DEER HUNTER'S TRUCK

DEER HUNTERS are an opinionated lot. I know; every year in camp I get an earful about the "ultimate" truck for deer hunters. Funny thing, though. No matter where I roam, the essential premise boils down to a pair of basic concerns: performance and storage. As one hunter put it, pulling on his red suspenders for emphasis, "There must be a way to get a truck that can crawl through the mud and climb steep trails and carry all my gear into camp—plus get my deer back home."

The search for this truck led to a joint venture that combined the talents of two very different companies: B&M Racing & Performance, and DeeZee. Initially, I feared the venture might become the ultimate clash of cultures—B&M is a West Coast high-performance company that cut its teeth on racing; DeeZee is a Midwest-based manufacturer run by hard-core hunters that built its reputation by designing and building heavy-duty running boards, grille guards, and storage and dog boxes.

But, like the fortuitous accident that yielded vulcanized rubber, B&M and DeeZee bonded instantly. That's because both understand the particular needs of the hunter.

The platform for the "ultimate" deer hunter's truck was a Ford F250. Because the truck was expected to carry huge loads into camp and see rugged offroad duty, it was equipped with B&M auxiliary engine oil and transmission oil coolers. To protect the front from offroad hazards, the truck was also fitted with DeeZee UltraBlack grille and brush guards.
P. Mathiesen

WEST COAST COOL

The platform for the project was a Ford F250 pickup. (Many deer hunters prefer $3/4$-ton pickups because of their greater load-carrying capability.) The truck had previously been fitted for serious offroad duty, so it was a natural choice for our upgrade.

Though I had no complaints about engine performance, I felt that the special demands of the deer hunter called for a transmission modification—one of B&M's specialties. Brian Appelgate of B&M told me, "Hunters stress transmissions in several ways. They usually carry huge loads into camp, and they often tow utility trailers. Guys who hunt in the mountains require their trucks to climb steep hills, and these trucks often see rugged offroad duty, including deep mud. All this creates heat, and heat is a certified transmission killer."

Hunters who wear suspenders and belts are no-nonsense types who take nothing for granted. The same philosophy guides B&M's recommendation for a pair of auxiliary coolers. The SuperCooler automatic transmission cooler and the SuperCooler engine oil cooler work together to keep the automatic transmission fluid and the engine oil nice and cool, even while the truck is pushed to the max.

B&M's second recommendation is designed to improve the performance of the automatic transmission. The ShiftPlus electronic shift improver kit electronically recalibrates the transmission's hydraulic system in order to eliminate "gear hunting." Doing so not only improves shift performance but helps to reduce heat buildup. The result is better performance and longer transmission life.

MIDWEST SOLUTIONS

From B&M I went to the folks at DeeZee. Ron Shivers, DeeZee's president, said, "There was a time when hunting trucks were hidden behind the house or sequestered in the garage. These trucks bore the scars of lots of offroad miles—the price of getting to out-of-the-way hunting sites. They did the job, but you didn't exactly want to be seen driving around town in 'em. Nowadays hunters need a 'hunting truck' to do double duty: The truck is often the family's main vehicle as well. To do that, you need to protect the truck from the scrapes, gouges, and dents that offroad trails inflict. That's why DeeZee developed running boards, grille guards, and the like.

"And truth be told, most hunters—me included—are gear freaks of the first order. Our storage boxes are designed to hold a lot of gear, so you can find it when you need it."

Shivers tackled the storage problem with a big box. "A haphazard pile of gear is no way to go," he said. "Let's go with our Platinum Series Fifth Wheel Tool Box."

Originally developed for outdoorsmen who use a fifth-wheel trailer, the tool box adapted easily to our needs. Constructed from heavy-duty Brite-Tread aluminum, the box bolts down to the bed. It features stainless steel paddle latches and heavy-duty gas cylinders. Since the top was designed to clear fifth-wheel hitches and trailers,

To hold the massive amount of gear that hunters bring to deer camp, DeeZee installed their Platinum Series Fifth Wheel Tool Box under the cap. It holds up to 25 cubic feet of gear.
P. Mathiesen

you'll have no trouble opening it in the tight space under a truck cap. The box holds up to 25 cubic feet of gear. I stuffed the box with two complete sets of bulky, cold-weather insulated hunting clothes, boots, sleeping bags, a pair of oversize gear bags, and miscellaneous camping equipment (gas lantern, stove, cooking utensils, etc.). It took a long time to fill.

To protect the vehicle from typical offroad hazards such as rocks, stumps, and brush, we installed the DeeZee UltraBlack grille bar and brush guards as well as Brite-Tread running boards. "Black is the hot choice among offroaders for grille and brush guards," Shivers said. "But chrome remains a favorite with a lot of hunters as well. It's really a matter of personal preference. The Brite-Tread diamond-plate aluminum running boards are an old favorite. They help you step up into the cab and protect the door and rocker panels from low obstacles. If you do a lot of really heavy-duty offroading, where the body of the vehicle comes into contact with mud or low brush, you might want to go with step bars instead because they'll give you a bit more clearance."

Shivers also addressed a prime concern for deer hunters: How to safely carry firearms. "Carrying firearms in a truck is always cause for worry. Getting jostled while in a soft case is the least of it. Most of us really worry that a much-needed stop for coffee late at night will give some creep the opportunity to rip off your rifles," he said.

DeeZee's Aluma-Sport Safari Gun Case is a heavy-duty extruded aluminum locking gun case that safely stores four rifles. A thick layer of foam padding protects rifles from jolts and bumps; no matter how bad the trail, you should still be zeroed in come opening day. For extra security, we bolted the case to the bed. The only way a thief will get the rifles is to steal the whole truck.

DeeZee's Aluma-Sport Safari gun case securely holds four rifles.
P. Mathiesen

FINAL TOUCHES

Once the B&M and DeeZee installations were completed, I went to Summit Racing Equipment (an Ohio-based supplier of mail-order performance parts) for three important additional contributions. First, they installed a Flowmaster cat-back exhaust. Improving the flow of exhaust gases helped the engine run more efficiently, which means we were able to put more power to the wheels, where it counts. (For more information on exhaust modifications, see Chapter 10.) Second, a Summit remote battery jump terminal (positive and negative posts) was mounted to the lower edge of the front bumper. When not needed, plastic caps protect each post. But if you need a jump start, instead of climbing under the hood and connecting directly to the battery, you attach the jumper cables to the remote terminal. This makes jump-starting faster and safer. Third, a Summit battery terminal disconnect switch allows you to separate the battery from the electrical system. This helps keep the truck from being hot-wired; it also means that if you leave the vehicle parked for a long time while in camp or on a day-long hunt, you won't have to worry that an accessory (such as a dome light) or some other electrical short will drain the battery.

That done, I called in the "Back Saver." The last time you hoisted a deer into the bed of the truck, did your back leave you writhing in agony? Well, next time let the Superwinch S4500 do the lifting. I mounted this compact winch to the bed, on top of a DeeZee cargo skid mat. (Originally designed to keep cargo from sliding around in the bed, the ribbed mat also hoses clean in seconds.) Now all you need to do is hook up the deer and have the S4500 do the work.

To ease back pain when hoisting a deer into the cargo bed, we installed a Superwinch S4500 light-duty winch to do the heavy lifting.
P. Mathiesen

Finally, I peered through the wheels and looked at the brakes. That prompted a call to The Progress Group (a California-based company that specializes in suspension and brake upgrades) for help. They recommended Extreme Performance brake pads and cross-drilled brake rotors. The system helps the front disc brakes dissipate heat more efficiently, which prevents brake fade (take note, high-country hunters). An additional benefit of cross-drilled rotors is that the brakes shed water more efficiently, which helps improve stopping power in wet conditions. The rear drum brakes received performance-lined brake shoes. (For more information on brakes upgrades, see Chapter 9.)

PART 2: THE "ULTIMATE" FISHING TRUCK

IF HE WERE in the movies, he'd be Gary Cooper or Harrison Ford. Their roles suit him to a "tee": the quiet man to whom everyone turns in a crisis. In other words, he's a natural.

Charley Cornelius grew up trout fishing; his father started him on the path when he was just 5 years old. And though he's now devoted to the fly rod, he's never outgrown his love of bait fishing, which may explain his delight in offending purists with tales of catching huge rainbows in Alaska with impaled field mice.

The first time we fished together in California's Sierra Nevada, Charley walked though a field kicking up grasshoppers that had yet to shed the morning dew. Each went into a small blue cricket basket. Later, while fishing a small creek, he crept noiselessly to an almost inaccessible pool. (The guy's got the knees of a 15-year-old.) As I

The platform for the "ultimate" fishing truck was a Ford F350, which featured a heavy-duty winch from Superwinch, auxiliary driving lights from IPF, and locking differentials from ARB.
E. Stewart

watched, he promptly caught three trout on three casts. His line placement through the tangle of limbs and brush was perfect.

Later in the afternoon, after I had pulled a nice rainbow out of a large plunge pool, he crept in behind me and extracted an enormous brown trout from the same water. He didn't yell or punch the air with his fist. The only way I knew he had a big one on was the way the rod bowed. Then he flashed a sheepish Cheshire-cat grin and patiently wore the fish down. When it was over, he looked the fish over quickly, backed out the fly (an olive Woolly Bugger), and put the brown back in the pool. His only comment: "Nice fish."

A former commercial airline and Alaska bush pilot who can mesmerize a group around a campfire with an endless stream of hilarious flying stories, Cornelius is also one of the most experienced offroaders I've ever seen. When the rear differential on one of our trucks blew out on a tough mountain trail, he winched the vehicle out. He just naturally assumed command and demonstrated the skills needed to extract the truck from a serious (let's call it a cliff-hanging) situation. The line pull was dicey, as the truck to be winched was sitting on the side of a talus slope. One wrong move, and it would tumble into a ravine. Once Cornelius sized up the situation, he went to work like a surgeon and deftly pulled the vehicle out of trouble.

That night, as we sat around the fire, I asked him about the unusual soft top on his truck.

"I call it the 'Can-Back,'" he said. "The canvas sides and rear flaps can be rolled up and secured for full access to the cargo bed. In addition, the frame and soft top can be removed and easily stored when you need the truck for work.

"The idea came out of my old Land Rover days," Charley continued. "You know, the old Land Rovers with soft tops? Well, in 1994 I bought an F350 4×4. My dog, Ruger, had always traveled in the back of my Land Rovers, and though the pickup worked well, the open bed didn't give Ruger any shade when I went fishing and camping in the mountains or offroading in the desert. I didn't need a hard cap, but that's all I could find on the market. Then I thought of those old Land Rover soft tops.

"So, I made the first Can-Back. Basically, it was an aluminum frame that I bolted to the bedrails of the pickup. Over that I placed a canvas cover that could fold up or down. That gave Ruger plenty of shade. It also gave me complete access to the entire bed, which you can't get with a hard cap.

The innovative cap is the "Can-Back," which allows full access to all parts of the cargo bed. Underneath is a custom rod rack.
E. Stewart

"I never saw dollar signs, but I soon realized I had something that people wanted. Guys just kept coming up to me and asking where I got 'that neat top.'"

Neat top indeed. The "canvas" is actually something called Sunbrella, a breathable fabric that carries a five-year guarantee against fading or loss of strength due to normal exposure to road conditions—including sunlight, mildew, rot, and atmospheric chemicals. A flurocarbon finish helps the fabric shed water.

In fact, the Can-Back offers functional flexibility without compromising durability or access. The complete kit consists of an extruded aluminum track system that bolts to the bedrails and a stainless steel superstructure on which the canvas cover is mounted. The structure is light in weight (60 pounds) but strong enough to support a full-size cargo rack capable of holding 300 pounds.

I was so impressed that I asked Charley to help me assemble a fishing truck, using his F350 as the base. What he devised is a reflection of his no-nonsense, practical nature. If he were a shotgun, he'd be a weathered pump—mechanically simple and utterly dependable.

Charley broke down the project into two main components: offroad performance and storage.

OFFROAD PERFORMANCE

Given Charley's offroad background, he wanted the truck to be able to get way back, "because the farther it can go, the better the fishing will be." True. But a heavy-duty offroad truck is also an asset in more "civilized" locales, such as muddy riverbottoms, slick steep boat ramps, and nasty dirt-and-gravel access roads to out-of-the-way impoundments.

First, Charley fitted the F350 with a rear manual locking differential and air compressor from ARB. (See Chapter 7 for a complete explanation of locking differentials.) The locking differential provides much-needed extra traction in rough spots; the air compressor inflates tires that have been aired down to run on beaches while you're fishing for striped bass or over slick rocks when chasing native cutthroats in the Rockies. The compressor also helps inflate float tubes and air mattresses.

The auxiliary driving lights came from IPF. Charley chose a discontinued model because he picked them up for a song. "Just because the lights were discontinued doesn't mean they weren't good. I saved a lot of money," he said. Good idea. Many mail-order and retail outlets offer great bargains on discontinued items. One word of caution, though. Invest in quality items only. Second-tier products—no matter how good the "savings"—aren't worth the money.

Charley is a big fan of manual transmissions. He feels he gets better fuel economy and offroad performance because he can select the precise gear required for the situation. That's why he ordered his F350 with the stock five-speed manual and the 7.5-liter big-block V8. Even so, he felt the engine could use a power boost, so he installed a performance chip. Doing so gave the engine about 10 percent more horsepower.

When it came to picking a winch, Charley remained with his Superwinch S9000, the winch used to pull the truck off the talus slope. As he says, "Break down one time in a place like this, and the winch pays for itself."

STORAGE

In the cargo bed, Charley stayed with his Can-Back top. On top of that he installed a custom roof rack with towers made from heavy-gauge steel that won't bend, flex, loosen, or rattle under severe offroad use; onto the rack went outsized Expedition Ballistic and heavy canvas gear bags sourced from Cabela's. On the inside frame he hung a custom rod rack of his own design. The full-size rack holds nine rigged rods and is made from heavy-duty aluminum and stainless steel. Each rod butt fits into closed-cell foam, while each tip is held in place by foam and elk hide.

Next in line was the Armadillo Truck Vault. This innovative slide-in

The Armadillo Truck Vault features two pull-out drawers and securely holds expensive graphite rods and other items.
E. Stewart

plywood storage compartment features two long locking drawers suitable for stowing expensive two-piece graphite rods as well as seven other storage boxes situated on the deck that can hold a variety of gear and tackle. When the vault is in place and the tailgate up, no one walking past will know your gear is even on board.

On top of the vault, Charley installed a livewell that consisted of a 48-quart marine cooler and a Super Fish Saver 12-volt aerator from Cabela's. When I kidded him about his passion for live bait, he said, "Sure, I still love fishing with live bait. You know why it's so important to start kids off this way? Because when they fish with live bait, they'll learn where the fish are—and that's information that stays with you for life, no matter how you fish later on."

Charley also went with a thermoelectric cooler from Coleman. The 32-volt unit plugs into the vehicle's cigarette lighter or any other 12-volt power outlet. It can cool without ice to 40 degrees below the ambient air temperature.

In the cab, Charley opted for a deluxe overhead console, Tough Guy cab organizer, and a deluxe car seat organizer—all from Cabela's.

Charley Cornelius reaches into livewell. Though primarily a flyfisherman, he still enjoys using live bait.
E. Stewart

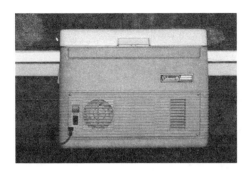

The Coleman thermoelectric cooler plugs into the vehicle's electric system. It provides ample cooling without ice.
E. Stewart

"I'm a very organized guy, and I hate climbing into messy trucks. It probably stems from my days as a pilot. Believe me, in an emergency you want to be able to find stuff in a hurry," he said.

Given the wide range of terrain and individual demands of hunters and fishermen, you may want to customize your truck in a different way. Fine. Just keep in mind that the "ultimate" truck does not require a quest that rivals the search for El Dorado. All you have to do is pick up the phone and ask for a catalog.

The Future of High Performance

The fate of the "computer" truck.

PART 1: THE LONG HAUL

K EITH PHILLIPS had a problem. At 126,000 miles, his 1991 Chevy K1500 4×4 pickup was beginning to show its age. Though the truck was basically in good shape, the 5.7-liter V8 engine seemed to lack the power needed to tow his bass boat, drive offroad while deer hunting, and haul loads for his home improvement business. He wanted to upgrade the engine's performance, but he also wanted the truck to run cooler and get a boost in fuel economy as well.

Fortunately, one of Phillip's hunting partners is Keith Stamper, owner of Pro-Motion Auto Machine, a Round Rock, Texas, performance shop. As a hunter, Stamper knows the kinds of performance that outdoorsmen want. "We're not talking drag-strip speed," he told me. "We're talking improvements in low-end torque for towing and offroad use without a penalty in fuel economy. Specifically, the trend in 4×4s seems to be leading toward exhaust and air intake systems, computer chips, and transmission upgrades. And since a lot of this stuff is computer controlled, we're doing a lot with the computer controls for both engines and transmissions."

THE "COMPROMISED" 4×4

Like millions of other truck-owning hunters and fishermen, Phillips drives a truck that has been compromised. By necessity, truck manu-

Outdoorsmen aren't looking for drag-strip speed when they begin a performance project. They're mainly interested in improved offroad and towing performance.
P. Mathiesen

facturers design pickups to appeal to a broad range of users. As a result, outdoorsmen often gripe that stock pickups don't deliver optimum towing and offroad performance. This is not a new complaint, and for years the automotive aftermarket has provided bolt-on products designed to improve engine efficiency.

What has changed over the past 20 years is the addition of on-board computers. And what we are learning fast is that bolt-on performance products (hardware) now need to work in tandem with the computer (software) in order to achieve optimum results.

JOINT EFFORT

Phillips elected to improve engine air intake by reducing exhaust back pressure. (The more efficiently an engine "breathes," the more

Modern performance modifications typically marry hardware (exhaust, for example) to software (performance chips) for best results.

power it can produce.) The obvious way to do this was to install headers as well as a cat-back exhaust, which would increase the truck's low- and mid-rpm torque output—the "grunt" power needed to get through mud, over rocks, and up steep boat ramps. To really maximize the benefits, Stamper also recommended installation of a Hypertech performance chip to create a complete hardware-software package. To maximize power from the increased air flow that the headers provide, Hypertech provided Power Tuning. This program has been designed specifically to complement the air flow changes of the headers and adjusts ignition spark and fuel delivery throughout the engine's power band.

The result? The power levels obtainable with the headers alone were roughly doubled through the addition of the Hypertech chip. The Chevy now boasts an additional 34 horsepower, achieved without a sacrifice in fuel economy. Also important, the power gains come in the low- to mid-rpm range, where it's needed most.

COOL RUNNINGS

Once the power problem was squared away, Stamper turned to the cooling system. Modern trucks are constantly battling heat, and running the air conditioning full tilt while towing in hot weather or grinding up steep offroad trails can tax the cooling system to the max. The transmission is also a factor; in fact, many boilovers are actually the result of hot transmission fluid overwhelming the vehicle's cooling system.

To combat heat, Stamper looked to products from B&M Racing & Performance, Flex-a-Lite, Summit Racing Equipment, and Design Engineering for the latest in cooling technology.

B&M contributed a SuperCooler auxiliary transmission cooler. The unit thwarts heat buildup in two ways: First, it enables you to use more automatic transmission fluid (ATF) to cool the transmission; second, the cooler's stacked plate design offers a larger surface area than conventional designs, which helps the unit dissipate heat faster.

B&M's TransPac valve body recalibration kit improves the quickness and firmness of the shift without loss of smoothness. The kit also significantly reduces clutch pack slippage. Slippage, familiar to drivers as "gear hunting," creates friction, and (remember your high school physics?) friction generates heat. Finally, a B&M temperature gauge is on board to monitor ATF temperature.

Flex-a-Lite's Black Magic 150 electric fan was designed to handle extreme heat by pulling more air through the radiator with less power consumption than stock equipment. (This gives you a performance benefit as well; typically, fans are parasites that siphon off power that could go to the wheels.) But the best benefit may be the fan's ability to move a large volume of air through the radiator whether you're ripping down the interstate, idling while a buddy checks a deer stand, or crawling through a rock field. All too often, outdoorsmen who operate 4×4s in hot weather have found that a big V8 engine will overheat while being driven at slow speeds because the stock fan simply can't pull in enough air to cool the engine.

From Summit Racing Equipment came a Howe replacement radiator (with a heat exchanger), specifically designed for high-temperature applications. The radiator not only holds more coolant, it uses it more efficiently to keep heat in check.

Finally, the Versa-Shield and Protect-A-Boot from Design Engineering insulate the starter and spark plug boots and wires from heat buildup. In the Chevy, Stamper used the Versa-Shield to protect the starter from heat soak. (A starter that gets too hot won't work until it has had time to cool off.) The Protect-A-Boot shields spark plug boots and wires from high heat buildup as well. This helps assure long life for the wires and plugs, and helps reduce the chance of misfires.

LONG RANGE

Texas sportsmen know all about long drives (the lyric "I've seen miles and miles of Texas" ain't no joke), but anyone who routinely drives long distances in remote areas knows the danger of running out of fuel. To counter this, Phillips—who often drives to New Mexico to hunt deer—wanted a larger fuel tank. Stamper recommended a 14-gauge aluminized steel (for superior rust resistance and strength) model, which mounts between the driver's side frame rail and the drive shaft. By moving from the 26-gallon stock tank to a 38-gallon tank, Phillips increased the range of the truck by 50 percent.

To make the long rides more bearable, Phillips also upgraded the tires. The design of the Uniroyal Laredo AWT light-truck tires strikes a good balance between on-road and offroad performance. The tires will also run much cooler on long runs than their beefy heavy-lugged offroad cousins—which helps ensure long tire life.

Since Phillips likes to hunt in rough, remote country, he wanted two final additions to his truck: auxiliary driving lights and a winch. Superwinch supplied the X9, which boasts a line-pull rating of 9,000 pounds and 100 feet of wire rope; and IPF recommended its RV Sports Series driving lights, as well as a halogen backup lamp.

By the time I got a chance to drive the revived Chevy, Phillips was ecstatic about the performance gains. "It's got a lot more pep," he said, "and I get better fuel economy to boot. I've really got a truck for the long haul."

Indeed he does. So do you. Don't think for a minute that you can't modify the modern "computer" truck. We may not be able to yank up the hood and dive in with a socket wrench the way we once did, but as the aftermarket learns to combine bolt-on hardware with plug-in software, we'll still be able to tweak our 4×4s.

After the field test, I told Phillips that I was impressed with the truck's overall appearance—particularly the body, which was in surprisingly good condition except for some scratches along the body panels.

"Are you going to get those taken care of?" I asked.

"Hell, no!" Phillips snorted. "Those are war wounds created by oak and mesquite branches. Around here we call 'em Texas pinstripes."

"What about that big scratch on the hood?"

Phillips laughed. "That's from when my buddy over here sighted in his gun. He forgot to put a pad down."

"Yeah," Stamper chipped in. "But I'm paying for it now. Every time we get stuck hunting, he makes me get out in the mud and run the winch."

PART 2: WHAT THE THUNDER SAID

THE MAIN INTERSECTION in the town in which I grew up was dominated by a firehouse and three gas stations. It could have been any intersection in middle America in the mid-1960s, and my first job was pumping gas at the Mobil station. Across the street, behind the firehouse, was our town's version of Gasoline Alley, a series of high-performance "speed" shops devoted to "The Embassy Trade" (we lived within shooting distance of Washington, D.C.), where a kid could hear the exotic, guttural roars of unmuffled Ferraris and Lamborghinis.

I also listened in wonder to American music every Friday evening as Tom, the chief mechanic, would peel out in his '55 Chevy, leaving twin streaks of black on the cement, and as Eddie, my fellow gas jockey, would rev his '66 Plymouth Satellite as he pulled it into a vacant service bay. He spent the summer, head under the hood, in a labor of love, and by Labor Day, through the addition of such high-performance components as a four-barrel carburetor, racing headers, glass packs, and high-performance manifolds, he had turned his 383-cubic-inch engine into one screamin' machine.

Back then, at the height of the muscle car era, the performance enthusiast was a marked man—a dirt-under-the-nails bruised-knuckles kind of guy. Essentially, he was dedicated to a single premise: "How do I make this thing go faster?" and he found a whole industry—based mainly in Southern California—ready to assist him in his quest.

But times change, and by the mid-1970s the glory days of the muscle car—and their sound of sweet thunder—were gone. Speed was replaced by caution and a new emphasis on fuel economy and emissions. Manufacturers realized that the mechanical systems that controlled a vehicle's performance could not deliver the precision that new government standards mandated. Slowly at first, and then with increasing speed, manufacturers began to incorporate electronic controls into their lines. Speed shop purists and shadetree mechanics grumbled: Every year it seemed there was less and less to work on.

Then, in the late 1980s, a funny thing happened on the way to the showroom. Trucks became cool. Long relegated to the "backwater" commercial and rural market, pickup trucks and sport utilities suddenly caught fire with suburban Baby Boomers who had tired of driving minivans. Outdoorsmen who had long known the virtues of

The mid-1970s Bronco remains a highly revered hunting vehicle, prized by many because it lacks any sort of computer controls. But vehicles from this period are not as mechanically reliable as newer 4×4s.

pickups and SUVs looked on in bemused wonder—until retail prices for "their" vehicles shot up because of the huge demand.

Now the modern truck is designed mainly for the suburbanite who, though he orders four-wheel-drive, may never take it off the pavement. Suspensions have been softened to make the vehicle more family friendly, and new engines designed for the masses can't do the jobs that sportsmen require of them.

All of this has spurred a renewed interest in "high performance" for 4×4s. Yet performance, as defined by the outdoorsman, does not mean drag-strip speed. It's a lot more than that. It's putting the ingredients together—say, a new manifold, electronics, upgraded transmission, and an exhaust system—in order to deliver more power for passing, towing, and climbing grades. What's important is that this improved performance and driveabilty comes in the low to mid-rpm range where outdoorsmen need it.

But while the outdoorsman of today has an unprecedented opportunity to custom-tune his truck to his type of hunting and fishing needs, many persist in the mistaken belief that the modern "computer truck" can't be worked on. Why?

Because of the "chip."

Welcome to the future, a world where the raspy whine of impact wrenches has gone the way of the steam shovel, replaced with the quiet hum of computer equipment. It's a brave new world that leaves many red-suspender outdoorsmen in the dark. And the focus of the old guard's ire is the so-called chip.

To find the role the chip plays in modern high-performance modification, I sat down with Mark Heffington, president of Hypertech, Inc., an innovative Memphis-based company that makes chips.

"Mark, just what do chips do?" I asked.

"Reduced to essentials, the chip is a tool that helps run the modern pickup," Heffington said. "Electronic systems that control the spark plugs to optimize performance have been around for years in the racing community. But in the early 1980s, General Motors began to install these systems in production vehicles; Ford and Chrysler soon followed suit. The advantage is that computer control systems allow very precise tuning under different types of conditions. Let me give you an example. During start-up, when engines are required to run rich, the air-fuel mixture ratio can be sufficiently enriched to prevent stumbling or stalling and spark curves can be optimized for extreme cold-start and rapid warm-up."

"I can remember my father pulling out the choke on our family sedan, and then waiting for what seemed an eternity for the car to warm up enough to run without stalling out," I said.

"Well, modern computer controls have eliminated that. I know many outdoorsmen don't like the idea of a computer truck, but the modern truck runs better—and longer—than any of those old trucks."

FEDERAL IMPETUS

What really got the ball rolling for on-board computer controls was pressure by the federal government for cleaner-running and more fuel-efficient vehicles. "On-board computer controls and emerging chip technology gave the truck manufacturers the ability to meet new government standards," Heffington said. "There was just one problem...."

The problem was that the manufacturers needed to build trucks that appealed to a wide and diverse market. Left out of the equation were those owners who needed their vehicles to serve special purposes—such as outdoorsmen who tow boats, haul heavy loads, or drive through deep troughs of mud. That opened the door to the aftermarket to supply chips that could customize a vehicle's performance to an individual's needs.

When computer-controlled engine management systems first came on the scene, chips—called Programmable Read Only Memory chips, or PROMs—could be unplugged and replaced, much like you'd change fuses in an electrical circuit. These devices contained ignition spark and fuel delivery information (calibrations) that could increase vehicle performance while still meeting more stringent emissions standards.

During this period, aftermarket chip manufacturers designed and built PROMs that could be dropped in, in place of the original equip-

Early performance chips were installed like fuses—just slipped in.
Hypertech

Modern chips are really sophisticated software packages that are downloaded into the truck's computer system.
Hypertech

ment manufacturer (OEM) PROMs. But over time OEM on-board computers evolved into what you see today: electronically erasable PROMs.

The advantage is that "these programs control an ever increasing number of engine and powertrain functions in an increasingly sophisticated way. These functions include air-fuel ratio, spark curves, transmission shift and lockup points, cooling fans, and even certain suspension controls. All of these capabilities can be tuned to fit the particular needs of a particular truck," Heffington said.

The disadvantage is that these sophisticated functions required another huge technological leap by the aftermarket suppliers, and chip installation now means downloading codes via a cable attached to the vehicle's computer.

BOTTOM LINE

"The bottom line for your guys is this: Don't think that you can't improve the performance of the modern computer truck," Heffington said. "You can. Sure, the tools have changed, but the basic idea hasn't. If you remember nothing else, remember this: A chip can help you in three basic ways. First, the majority of the gain is improved fuel economy. Who's going to argue with that? Second, the chip improves towing ability, and it also helps the vehicle perform better offroad. Third, it helps the vehicle deliver improved acceleration and performance overall."

If the chip can deliver all that, then why are there still so many Doubting Thomases? Apart from the fact that many of us instinctively shrink from the new, one of the major stumbling blocks to the acceptance of high-performance chips is the fear that such modifications will void the warranty—a fear often played up by truck dealers.

Electronic computer control systems first made their appearance in vehicles made by General Motors in the early 1980s.

Despite what the service manager at your dealership may tell you, such modifications are completely legal—and protected by federal law—as long as you use parts that have been certified by the Environmental Protection Agency. If the dealer gives you a hard time, stand your ground. Your truck is legal, your warranty valid.

A couple of years ago, a truck performance expert told me, "No question, electronics is a whole new ballgame for a lot of people in the automotive aftermarket. It's an extreme challenge. And if you can't conquer it, then you might as well forget everything else— because no matter how good the other pieces are, if you can't make them work with the computers on these trucks, you can't deliver better performance."

But the aftermarket is meeting the challenge. So, when I hear a friend moan about the "good old days of burnt rubber and sweet thunder," I tell him the "good old days" are right now. Here's what the thunder said to me: You want a truck that can handle deep-rutted

The industry moved quickly to adapt electronic controls, and by the late 1980s most trucks were equipped with some form of electronic engine management.

Though some auto dealers claim that modifications to new trucks and sport utilities will void the warranty, performance modifications are completely legal, as long as you use parts that have been certified by the Environmental Protection Agency.

trails? *Done.* You want a truck that can tow a loaded trailer up to an alpine deer camp? *Done.* You want a truck that burns less fuel, but delivers more performance? *Done.* You want a truck that effortlessly pulls a fully loaded bass boat up a steep, slick boat ramp? *Done.*

The only difference now is that we don't get our hands dirty—unless, of course, we're trying to pull a nightcrawler out of a Styrofoam cup for a favorite nephew who believes his uncle is just the guy to help him catch his first big bass.

Appendix

T
HE FOLLOWING SECTION is a compendium of products, advice, and a manufacturer resource list designed to help you get more out of your 4×4.

1. BODY RESTORATION

Although most buyers of old trucks aren't interested in restoring the body and paint to showroom specs, repairing any body damage is a high-priority task. Fortunately, you don't need previous experience with body or paint restoration; your local auto parts store usually carries a full line of restoration products (with instructions) designed for the do-it-yourselfer. You'll also be relieved to learn that the job requires a minimum of tools, thus reducing the financial investment.

First, thoroughly clean the outside of the truck, using cleaning products specially formulated for vehicles. (Dish-washing liquids and other household detergents won't cut the mustard.) Then use a tar and bug remover to remove silicones, wax, and grease. That done, you can tackle the first repair—minor rust spots. This job calls for sanding discs, sandpaper, body filler, and primer, all available from the local auto parts store.

Grind off the rust, taking the paint down to bare metal. Then drill holes around the spot where the rust used to be. These holes hold an adhesive-backed body repair screen. Once that is in place, apply body filler, shape and sand down the patch, and apply primer. The trick here is to wet-sand the primer with a water-filled sponge and extra-fine sandpaper.

Next on the list: scratches. After the surface has been cleaned, use a very fine sandpaper and wet-sponge to feather-edge the scratch. This will be tough at first. You need to get a gradual taper from the old paint to the bare metal so the repair will look right. The job is done when you can run your fingers over the scratch without feeling the edge. It will take a while to get the right touch.

Once a scratch has been feather-edged, apply primer and spot putty and sand as needed. For best results when painting, mask the area 3 inches past the repair to allow for good coat blending. Apply the primer and final color, then sand with 1,000-grit wet sanding paper to enhance the final appearance. Use rubbing compound to increase the shine.

The biggest challenge is saved for last: body dents. This job ordinarily requires a specialized slide hammer (used by body shops to pull out dents), but there is a more cost-effective way to do this. Drill a $1/16$-inch hole in the center of the dent and insert a metal screw into the hole; then grip the screw with a pair of pliers and pull out the dent. Sand and grind the area to remove any rust, then fill in with body filler. Sand the filler, mask the area, and apply primer. Sand and feather-edge the area before you apply the final coat of paint.

After dents, check the paint on your vehicle. If the paint has been oxidized by exposure to years of hot sun, you may initially feel the only recourse is a complete paint job—an expensive proposition. There's a cheaper way, however. Stop by your local auto parts store and ask the counterman to recommend a good fine-cut rubbing compound and cleaner wax. The pair work together to remove the top layer of oxidized (chalky) paint as well as all gunk and grime. Most experts recommend a good orbital sander or rotary buffer for this type of work, but you can make do with a 5-inch buffer on a variable-speed electric drill. Go slowly, though, or you might burn right through the paint to the primer.

When you're through, a buddy who casts a knowing eye along the body might see warps and ridges from the body filler, but who cares? You still did a nice job, at a fraction of the cost of professional body restoration. This is a good example of the type of job that is worth every penny in sweat equity. Take the money you save here and invest it in areas that really require the professional touch.

2. Mail Order Made Easy

Truck accessories are big business. And though many outdoorsmen continue to buy parts at retail outlets, each year more are letting their fingers do the walking by ordering aftermarket accessories from mail-order companies. This approach is convenient, but pitfalls abound for the unwary. If you prefer to shop via telephone and credit card, the wise course is to observe "The Three Rules of Mail Order," as promulgated by Joel Fischel, customer service representative for Summit Racing Equipment, an Ohio-based high-performance mail-order outfit.

Know Your Truck

"Rule number one, know your truck," says Fischel. "The more you know about your truck and the parts you want to install, the better. One of the most common problems in mail order is that potential customers often don't even know the kind of truck they own.

"We talk to customers every day who don't know if their truck is a Ford or a Chevy. I'm not kidding. They don't know the size of the engine, whether the truck is a short-bed or long-bed. If you don't know your truck, there's no way you can order accessories intelligently."

Does It Fit?

"Rule number two, know how new accessories will effect the performance of your truck. For example, tire upgrades are one of the most common changes a truck owner makes. But if you go to a larger tire without changing the differential gears, you're going to lose power. Then, when you hit a tough section of hilly trail, you'll wonder why the truck can't cut it. And bogging down here can also burn up the engine as well as the transmission."

Package Power

"Rule number three, try to put together a package deal. Most mail-order outfits will offer a deep discount to the guy who is going to spend a lot of money. If you've done your homework and know what you need, the most efficient—and in the long run cheapest—way is to order it all at one time. Yes, it's a big hit, but you'll save on freight charges as well as the cost per item. Buying parts piecemeal is the most expensive way to customize your truck."

3. HI-LIFT JACK

Conceived in the horse and buggy era, the Hi-Lift Jack has changed little in nearly a century. It remains one of the most useful and versatile tools for the hunter or fisherman who ventures off the beaten track.

The key to the Hi-Lift Jack's enduring popularity is its extraordinary simplicity and functionality. It can lift, hoist, winch, clamp, push, and pull—which means it can handle a wide range of offroad emergencies, from freeing a 4×4 from rocks and mud to popping the bead on a flat tire. In addition, the jack can be scooted under bumpers as low as $4^1/_2$ inches from the ground (which occurs when the axles are buried in mud), and the 37-inch lift range gives you ample room to lift a vehicle off a large rock.

A monument to old-fashioned solid construction, the jack consists of an upright steel bar, a top clamp (for winching or hoisting), a base, a lifting mechanism, a two-piece handle, and socket. A pair of climbing pins located on the steel bar raise or lower a load, and a safety shear pin keeps an operator from overloading the jack. (If a load exceeds the 7,000-pound capacity, the shear pin will break without dropping the load.)

Driven on arm power, the jack might tire you out during a long session. On the other hand, there are no batteries, wire connections, relays, or other modern marvels to impede operating performance.

All of the winch's operations—vertical and horizontal—use the same basic lifting procedures. To raise a 4×4, place the handle of the jack in the upright position against the steel bar. Place the base on firm, level ground. (In mud, use a 2×2-foot section of wood to support the base.) Position the lifting nose under the vehicle, then engage the reversing latch. Pull up on the handle so the lifting mechanism will slide along the bar until the nose is secured under the bumper. (If the vehicle doesn't have a bumper, make sure the nose rests against the frame or a solid attachment such as a side bar. Don't position the nose under suspension parts or plastic trim.) Now grab the handle with both hands and pump to raise the load.

The lifting mechanism literally walks up the bar courtesy of a pair of heavy-duty climbing pins. When the handle is pushed down, the top pin is released from the bar and the weight is transferred to the bottom pin. The top pin travels upward about 1 inch and clicks back into the bar. As the handle is drawn up, the weight of the load shifts back to the pin, releasing the bottom pin. It's simple, and utterly dependable.

To lower the jack, place the handle in the upright position against the bar and push the reversing latch to the down position. Grasp the handle with both hands and pump down. The pressure will now be on the up stroke, so hold on tight.

Winching is equally simple. Attach one end of a chain to the vehicle's tow hook or frame; the other end of the chain fastens to the end of the jack's lifting nose. Attach another chain or tow strap to the jack's top clamp and then rig to a solid anchor point. (If you use a tree, make sure to use a nylon tree-saver strap).

Lift the reversing latch, take out the slack, and start pumping the handle. The process will be slow going compared to an electric winch but ultimately no less effective. If you have to winch a long distance, use a wheel chuck to keep the vehicle in place (so you don't lose any hard-won ground) while you reset the chains for another pull.

The jack can also be used for more specialized offroad situations. If you need to fix a flat on a large offroad tire, the jack can be used to break the bead on the tire. Place the flat underneath a jacking point on the 4×4 and set the base of the jack on the tire's sidewall. Engage the reversing latch, lift up the nose, and start pumping the handle—just as if you were going to raise the truck. The bead will pop after a few strokes.

If you roll into a boulder and crush a fender on a tire, use the jack to pull the sheet metal far enough off the tire to get home. The base and the nose of the jack can deliver 7,000 pounds of spreading force—more than enough to give the tire some breathing room.

Keep the jack clean and lubricated, as accumulated grit and grime can jam the climbing mechanism. For best results, clean and spray lubricant on the pins and bar after every use. Inspect the climbing pins occasionally for excess wear and tear.

When you first heft a Hi-Lift Jack, the heavy weight will surprise you. That's because it's made of heavy cast steel, which gives the jack the feel of another era. Nothing wrong there—it works. For more information, contact Hi-Lift Jack, 46 W. Spring St., Bloomfield, IN 47424-0228, www.hi-lift.com.

4. Essential Information

Gauges providing such vital information as fuel level, charging system, oil pressure, and coolant temperature are standard factory equipment in most trucks. But outdoorsmen who tow need more information than what these gauges can deliver. If you haul really heavy loads or if you tow a boat, invest in quality aftermarket gauges. In particular, I recommend gauges that monitor three key areas: automatic transmission fluid temperature, engine oil temperature, and vacuum.

Why these three? The two that track heat were selected because modern truck engines generate a great deal of heat. If the engine or transmission can't shed that heat properly, it will self-destruct, so gauges that tell you the operating temperatures of the engine oil and transmission fluid can save your vehicle's life. The vacuum gauge isn't quite as vital, but it can save you fuel—almost as valuable an asset.

Transmission

The automatic transmission fluid (ATF) is the lifeblood of one of the most complex and expensive components in your 4×4. When towing, the increased loads on the transmission—the torque converter, in particular—can raise the temperature of the ATF to damaging levels. Being able to constantly monitor the ATF temperature can tell you about a developing problem before it becomes catastrophic. A much underrated benefit of this gauge is to ensure proper warmup: You can see when the fluid temperatures reach normal levels. Heavy loading should be avoided until this point.

Engine Oil

Most trucks come from the factory with oil pressure gauges. These gauges tell you that something in the lubrication is preventing the oil from reaching vital engine parts. So far, so good. But significant engine damage can occur before oil pressure is affected.

That's where an engine oil temperature gauge can save your bacon. A sharp spike in the temperature of the engine oil serves as an early warning that trouble is on the way.

The ability to monitor oil temperature also helps ensure long engine life. About one-third of the engine's cooling comes from the oil itself, so if you can detect hot-running oil early enough, you can have the problem corrected before it becomes a major repair.

Vacuum

Looked at one way, the engine is an air pump. A vacuum gauge records the difference in air pressure between the atmosphere and the partial vacuum created in the intake manifold as each piston moves down on the intake stroke.The gauge is calibrated in inches of mercury, usually from 0 to 30. Low vacuum indicates high throttle (increased fuel consumption); high vacuum means low throttle (decreased fuel consumption.)

But all you really need to know about a vacuum gauge is that it can help you improve fuel economy by as much as 20 percent.The higher the reading, the better the fuel economy, so it pays to keep the needle on the high side. Backing off the throttle during low-vacuum (high-throttle) conditions not only helps reduce fuel consumption, but it also lessens the strain on the drivetrain, often while maintaining virtually the same speed.

Installation

Gauge placement is crucial. For best results, gauges should be readily visible, so you don't have to move your head any great degree; at the same time, the gauges should not obstruct the view over the hood or of other controls and instruments. Usually, you can put gauges on the extreme left-hand side of the dashboard, near the windshield, where they will be visible but out of the way.Another good spot is the flat spot (if any) on the dashboard above the radio.

5. The Keys to Vehicle Security

As many owners of 4×4s have learned the hard way, the boom in the four-wheel-drive pickup and sport-utility market has also spawned a lucrative black market in stolen vehicles. Sportsmen are especially hard hit because many thieves know that these rigs often contain special goodies (firearms) that can be converted to ready cash.

A security consultant once told me, "Look, you can't stop a pro. If he wants your truck, he'll get it—even if it's locked up in Fort Knox. What you can do is protect the vehicle from the semi-pro and talented amateur.

"The first step is simple. Lock the vehicle. You wouldn't believe how many people still don't bother to do this. And never leave the keys in the ignition. That's also something too many people still do. It sure isn't tough to steal a truck if all the thief has to do is climb behind the wheel and drive off.

"The next step is to set up a line of defense. You want to make the thief pause. If you can get him to do that, he'll most likely move on to easier pickings. What makes it tough for your guys is that they park in out-of-the-way spots where prying eyes can get a good long look at the prize."

So how do we make a thief pause? By erecting a series of barriers that cost him time. Over the years I've seen all sorts of home remedies, ranging from welding angle iron across doors to hiding gear under old blankets covered with garbage. Such tactics may work with older trucks that can be devoted exclusively to hunting and fishing, but they're inappropriate if your 4x4 must also serve double duty as a family vehicle.

The best approach is a two-tier plan that emphasizes cost-effectiveness and simplicity.

The first tier is vehicle immobilization. This narrows the field to an ignition-cutoff switch. Unfortunately, most models utilize switches that tuck under the dashboard and are easily found by thieves. I also prefer a heavy-duty component that can stand up to the rigors of offroad use and the wet conditions that we hunters and fishermen encounter.

The product that has worked best for me is a cutoff switch from Flaming River, 17851 Englewood Dr., Cleveland, OH 44130, www.flaming-river.com. The device is spliced into the truck's electrical system; when activated, it completely disconnects the electrical system, which keeps the engine from getting any spark. This has a nice side benefit as well. By disconnecting the electrical system, you'll keep the battery from being drained by a short circuit.

The switch's special feature is a removable key that you take with you. Even if the thief locates the switch, he can't deactivate it.

The second tier involves a system that can help keep such expensive and much-in-demand components as wheels, spare tires, and pickup tailgates from being ripped off. In this instance the folks at McGard, 3875 California Rd., Orchard Park, NY 14127, www.mcgard.com., came to the rescue.

McGard locks are made from a high-strength steel alloy that resists tampering. The "key" to each lock is a computer-designed puzzle lock. For wheels, you install one lock per wheel (in place of one of the lug nuts). Outside-mounted spares can be fitted with a wheel lock; underbody spares can also be protected by fitting the lock to the underbody storage housing. Another lock uses the same technology to keep the tailgate from being lifted out of the bed.

As you've no doubt noticed, this approach to vehicle security is based on keys. Going this route delivers good security at a reasonable cost, and it doesn't rely on high-tech components that can't take the rigors of woods and waters. Unfortunately, part of the price is a certain loss of convenience—especially for anyone who habitually misplaces keys. But it's a trade-off that can't be avoided. Think of the alternative.

6. ON TOP

Pickup truck owners may be divided into two classes: those who prefer to leave the cargo bed open, and those who prefer to cover the bed with a cap. Caps protect your hunting and fishing gear from the elements and provide some measure of security.

Pickup caps come in two basic flavors—aluminum and fiberglass. Aluminum caps are inexpensive and generally appeal to the outdoorsman on a tight budget. Fiberglass caps cost more, but look better, usually flush-mount for a more aerodynamic fit (which saves fuel in the long run), and can be color-matched to the pickup's factory paint. Models usually feature a sliding-window option (so the driver or passenger can reach into the cargo bed from the cab), locks, and an interior light. The light may be hard-wired to the vehicle's electrical system or use batteries.

The Achilles' heel of nearly every cap—no matter how well it is designed and constructed—is the locking system. If you live in the Northern tier of states, road salt will foul the locks within a couple of seasons. When this happens, take the rig to a good locksmith and have him replace the lock cylinders with corrosion-resistant models. Not all locksmiths carry such a line, so you may have to make a few calls, but it will be worth it.

7. ROOF RACKS

Roof racks come in two general styles: the tower systems made popular by such brands as Thule and Yakima, and the so-called "Safari" style such as those made by Surco and Garvin. The former features posts that lock into a vehicle's drip rails (internal or external) via a C-clamp design and a crossbar (round or rectangular), to which a wide assortment of accessories (including canoes, johnboats, and mountain bikes) can be attached. The other major advantage is that these racks are not permanent installations; they can be removed and stored in the garage or shed when not needed.

The Safari style generally bolts to the roof of a sport utility (though some can be attached to external drip rails) or to the cap on a pickup. This type of rack features high-rise sides that can securely hold a massive amount of gear. The disadvantage (to some sportsmen) is that Safari racks are permanent installations.

But where there's a will, there's a way. I was striper fishing one morning when I saw a Dodge Raider (a compact two-door SUV) parked on the beach. The owner had outfittd his truck with a special front-bumper rack that held a cooler for bait; he had mounted a Surco rack on top. But I noticed something different. The rack was supported with Yakima towers that clamped to the exterior drip rails. I pointed this out to the owner, who said, "I didn't like the Surco permanent mounts, and I wanted to make the rack removable. So I jerry-rigged the Yakima towers to fit the Surco rack. It was easy to."

The choice of rack ultimately depends on your personal preference. Keep in mind one important fact, however. The amount of weight a rack can handle is really determined by how much the roof (on a sport utility) or a cap (on a pickup) can handle. Consult the respective manufacturer first to see how much weight your vehicle can really bear.

8. THE CLEAN MACHINE

It is said, "Rust never sleeps." Believe it, especially if you are the owner of a 4×4 that sees mud, water, and salt. Left alone to do its dirty work, rust will reduce your rig to a heap of unsightly scrap in a surprisingly short time.

Coastal and snowbelt sportsmen are particularly at risk, but any outdoorsman who takes his vehicle into wet environments needs to know how to combat corrosion. "Wet" environments can be found in surprisingly dry places, too, so just because you live outside a high-risk area is no reason to breathe easy. As an example, the dove hunter who routinely drives into fields for the afternoon flight can run into trouble if he fails to clear out any matted grass from under the chassis. Left in place, that grass can act as a moisture trap.

The remedy is as simple as it is effective: cleanliness.

As soon as you get home from a hunting or fishing trip, wash off any mud and dirt from the body. Then get down on your knees and wash off the crud underneath the vehicle. Pay special attention to the wheel wells, as this is usually where rust goes to work first.

One of my hunting buddies places an oscillating-type lawn sprinkler on the driveway and then slowly drives back and forth over it. The pressure isn't enough to loosen entrenched mud and crud, but at least it washes off road film and salt.

If the vehicle is particularly muddy, drive to a coin-operated commercial washer and use the high-pressure hose to blast out the mud and crud. Do this before the mud has a chance to dry to a hard cake.

If you've been four-wheeling in deep mud troughs, pull the wheels and inspect the brakes and brake lines. I failed to this after a week-long deer hunt in muddy terrain, though I had at least hosed off the vehicle with a high-pressure spray the day I headed home. In spring I noticed something wrong with the brakes and took it to the shop. When the mechanic gave me the bill, I nearly fainted. The front disc brakes were ruined. I had never removed the mud from the brakes, and it acted as a corrosive water trap all winter long.

So, it really does pay to keep your 4×4 clean.

9. Aftermarket Manufacturer Resource List

ALCOA WHEEL PRODUCTS
  INTERNATIONAL
1600 Harvard Ave.
Cleveland, OH 44105
800-242-9898
www.alcoawheels.com
*Forged aluminum wheels and
  accessories for light trucks*

AUTOCOM, INC.
8408 Danville Dr.
Austin, TX 78753
512-833-8813
jmcfarl@aol.com
Consulting and product design

ARB 4×4 ACCESSORIES, INC.
20 S. Spokane St.
Seattle, WA 98134
206-264-1669
www.arb.com.au
Locking differentials

A.R.E. INC.
400 Nave Rd.
Massillon, OH 44648
800-824-9561
www.4are.com
Fiberglass truck caps

B&M RACING & PERFORMANCE
 PRODUCTS, LLC
9142 Independence Ave.
Chatsworth, CA 91311
818-882-6422
www.bmracing.com
*Performance transmission
 products*

CABELA'S OUTFITTERS
One Cabela Dr.
Sidney, NE 69160
www.cabelas.com
*Mail-order and retail hunting, fish-
 ing, and camping gear*

CAN-BACK, INC.
9649 Remer St.
South El Monte, CA 91733
877-SOFT-TOP
www.can-back.com
*Soft caps and custom roof racks
 and rod holders*

THE COLEMAN COMPANY
3600 N. Hydraulic
Wichita, KS 67219
800-835-3278
www.coleman.com
Camping equipment

DEEZEE, INC.
P.O. Box 3090
Des Moines, IA 50316-0090
800-779-2102
www.deezee.com
*Running boards, toolboxes, tail-
 gate protectors, mud flaps, bed-
 caps, rails, grille guards, sport
 bars, hood shields*

DRAW-TITE, INC.
40500 Van Born Rd.
Canton, MI 48188
800-521-0510
www.draw-tite.com
*Trailer hitches and towing acces-
 sories*

FLOWMASTER, INC.
2975 Dutton Ave.
Santa Rosa, CA 95407-7800
707-569-9929
www.flowmastermufflers.com
*Performance mufflers and exhaust
 systems*

GOODRIDGE (USA), INC.
20309 Gramercy Pl.
Torrance, CA 90501
800-662-2466
www.goodridge-usa.com
Performance brakelines

HYPERTECH, INC.
3215 Appling Rd.
Bartlett, IN 38133-3999
901-382-8888
www.hypertech-inc.com
*High-performance power chips,
 power modules, power pro-
 grammers, and related accessories*

IPF
20 S. Spokane St.
Seattle, WA 98134
206-264-1669
www.arb.com.au
Auxiliary driving lights

MICHELIN NORTH AMERICA
(UNIROYAL)
1 Pkwy. S.
Greenville, SC 29602-9001
846-458-6177
www.uniroyal.com
High-performance light-truck tires

POWERSTOP/AUTOSPECIALTY
800 E. 230th St.
Carson, CA 90745
800-275-2377
www.autospecialty.com
Performance brake products

THE PROGRESS GROUP
1390 N. Hundley St.
Anaheim, CA 92806
800-905-6687
www.progressauto.com
*Manufacturer and distributor of
performance springs and
related suspension products*

SUMMIT RACING EQUIPMENT
P.O. Box 909
Akron, OH 44309-0909
800-230-3030
www.summitracing.com
*Distributor and manufacturer of
performance automotive products and truck accessories*

SUPERWINCH, INC.
45 Danco Rd.
Putnam, CT 06260-3001
860-928-7787
www.superwinch.com
*Electric winches, grille guards, and
winch accessories*

SURCO PRODUCTS, INC.
14001 S. Main St.
Los Angeles, CA 90061
800-345-1704
Roof racks

TRAILMASTER SUSPENSION
420 Jay St.
Coldwater, MI 49036-9497
800-832-4847
*Light-truck suspension compo-
nents, including shock
absorbers, springs, and steering
components*

TRUCK VAULT
211 Township St.
Sedro Woolley, WA 98284
800-967-8107
www.truckvault.com
*Storage units for pickups and
sport utilities*

10. Log Book (See Chapter 3.) Photocopy the form and keep it handy in the glovebox.

Glove Box Log

Date _____

Mileage Before _____

Mileage After _____

Weather_____

Destination/Route _____

_____

_____

Towing _____ Weight _____

Vehicle Comments _____

_____

_____

Trip Notes_____

_____

_____

Follow-up _____

_____

_____

11. USED-4×4 CHECKLIST (See Chapter 2.) Photocopy the form and take it with you when you look for a used 4×4.

Vehicle Information

Year _____ Model _____

Engine _____ Mileage _____

Body

Component	Condition	Comments

Interior

  Seats

  Mirrors

Glass

  Windshield

  Side Windows

  Rear Window

Exterior

  Paint

  Trim

  Dents

  Bumpers

Other (List)

Mechanicals

Component	Condition	Comments

Exterior

   Headlamps

   Auxiliary Lights

   Wipers & Washers

   Transmission

   Brakes

   Wheels

   Shock Absorbers

   Springs

   Tires

   Steering

Interior

   Turn Signals & Flasher

   Horn

   Heater/AC

Under the Hood

Fluids

   Engine Oil

   Transmission Fluid

Component	Condition	Comments
Coolant/Antifreeze		
Brake Fluid		
Drive Belts		
Battery		
Air Filter		

Index

4×4s, *see* Sporting vehicles
4WD, *see* Four-wheel drive

Acceleration, 22, 44
Accessories, 9-10, 115-16
  inspecting, 19
  mail order, 160-61
  manufacturers of, 169-71
  transmission, 71-72
Airbeds, 123
Air compressors, 145
Airing down, 42
Air springs, auxiliary, 33-34
Aluminum
  caps, 167
  wheels, 46-49
American Petroleum Institute (API)
  oil rating system, 132
Anchor points, for winches,
    100-101, 163
Antifreeze, 136
Anti-lock brake systems (ABS),
    82-84
Auctions, used-vehicle, 25-26
Automatic transmission fluid (ATF),
    69-70, 74-75, 136, 164
Auxiliary driving lights, 145, 152
  buying tips, 94-95
  electrical system and, 94
  government regulations
    regarding, 92
  positioning, 93-94
  wattage of, 94
Axle(s)
  locking, 62

ratio, 75
submerging of, 67

Back pressure, 86, 87
Baffles, in mufflers, 88
Balance, 34
Ball joints, 28
Battery jump terminals, remote, 141
Bearings, 67
Bellows type, of leaf-spring applica-
    tions, 33
Body restoration, 159-60
Bounce test, 28
Brake(s), 77-84
  corrosion of, 169
  drums, 80-81, 142
  friction and, 79-80
  heat and, 78
  inspection, 22
  lines, 81-82, 169
  locking, 82-84
  pads, 79-80, 142
  pedal feel, 79-80
  rotors, 80-82, 142
  shoes, 79, 142
  tires and wheels and, 78
  traction and, 82-84
  upgrading, 79-82, 142
Braking, 44-45, 114
Brush guards, 140
Bumpstops, 29, 30
Bushings, 28, 29-30

Camp boxes, 125
Camp coolers, 146

Camping, 120-27
Can-Back, 143-44
Canoes, 127
Caps, 167
Cargo beds, 167
Catalytic heaters, 126
Cat-back exhaust systems, 87, 141,
    150
Chairs, camp, 125-26
Clutch, 22
Coil-spring applications, 33
Combustion efficiency, 85, 86
Computers, 41, 58, 145, 149, 150,
    153, 154-58
Connectors, 107-108
Coolant, 21, 136
Corrosion, 18-19, 112, 168-69
Cylinder pressure, 20, 21

Dealers, 10-11
    auctions, 25-26
    used-vehicle, 10-11, 25
Deer hunters, trucks for, 137-42
Dents, 160
Department of Transportation
    (DOT) standards, 82
Differential(s), 61-67
    full-locking, 62-66
    limited-slip rear, 61, 62
    locking rear, 62, 145
    "open," 61-62
Dipsticks, 136-37
Doors, 19
Driveline components, 18

Emissions standards, 8, 153
Engine(s), see also Oil
    inspection, 20-21
    overhead-camshaft, 8
    pushrod, 8
    size, 7
Environmental Protection Agency,
    157
Equipment, see Accessories

Exhaust system(s), 18
    cat-back, 87
    heat and, 89
    manifold, 86
    noise from, 22
    upgrading, 85-89

Fans, radiator, 151
Fatigue, 18
Fiberglass caps, 167
Filters
    oil, 128, 130, 131
    transmission, 69, 72
Firearms, 140
Fishing, trucks for, 142-47
Flashlights, 126, 127
FMVSS (Federal Motor Vehicle Stan-
    dards System), 106, 81-82
Fog lamps, 91-92
Food, 123-25, 127
Four-wheel drive
    engagement of, 8-9, 22
Frame, 18
Fuel consumption, 8, 153
    gear ratios and, 55-56, 59
Fuel tanks, 151

Gauges, 163-65
    oil pressure, 164
    oil temperature, 164
    placement of, 165
    temperature, see Temperature
        gauges
    vacuum, 165
Gear ratios, 54-56, 58-60, 66, 75
Gears
    for hill climbing, 119
    oil, 67
    tire size and, 53, 57-58
Government regulations
    auxiliary lights, 92
Government standards, 8, 153, 155
Grille bars, 140
Grills, 126

Gross axle weight rating (GAWR), 105
Gross combined weight rating (GCWR), 105
Gross trailer weight (GTW), 105
Gross vehicle weight (GVW), 73
Gross vehicle weight rating (GVWR), 33, 104-105
Gun cases, 140

Headers, 86, 150
Headlights
  auxiliary driving lights and, 93-94
  halogen, 90
Heat, 150-51, *see also* Temperature gauges
  brakes and, 78
  exhaust systems and, 89
  fluids and, 136, *see also* under Automatic transmission fluid (ATF); Oil
  stop-and-go traffic and, 74
  towing and, 73-74
  transmissions and, 69, 70, 74
  weight and, 74
High stands, 126
Hill climbing, 119
Hitches, 104-12, *see also* Towing; Trailers
  balls, 107
  classes of, 106-107
  installation, 9
  step-bumper, 107
  weight-carrying, 106
  weight-distributing, 106, 107
Hubs, locking, 8-9

Ignition cutoff switch, 166
International Lubricant Standardization and Approval Committee (ILSAC), 131-32

Jacks, 162-63
Jump starting, 141

Kelley Blue Book, 24
Keys, 167
Knock, 21

Lanterns, 126, 127
Leaf-spring applications, 33
Leaks, 18
Lift kits, 34-36
Lights, 19, *see also* Flashlights; Fog lamps; Headlights; Lanterns
  auxiliary, *see* Auxiliary driving lights
  for trailers, 112
Load carrying, 32
  of tires, 42
Load hauling, *see also* Towing
  brake rotors and, 81
Load leveling, 33
Load rating
  wheels and, 50
Locking axles, 62
Locking hubs, 8-9
Locks, 166-67
Logbooks, 30-31, 172

Mail order, of accessories, 160-61
Maintenance schedules, 66-67, 130
Modifications
  legality of, 156-57
Mufflers, 87-89
Muscle cars, 153

Noise
  exhaust system, 22
  performance vs., 87-88

Offroad driving, 43-45, 113-19, *see also* Hill climbing; Trails
  braking in, 82-84
  long drives, 151-52
Oil
  additives, 133
  changing, 128-31

Oil *(continued)*
  climate and, 133–34
  designations, 131–32
  dipsticks, 136–37
  function of, 131–32
  gauges, 164
  gear, 67
  synthetic, 135
  transmission, 71, 74, *see also*
    Automatic transmission fluid
    (ATF)
  viscosity, 133–35
  volatility, 135
On-board computers, *see* Computers
On Board Diagnostic (OBD) system,
  58

Paint, 18, 160
Performance chips, 145, 150
Pickups, *see also* Sporting vehicles
  engines in, 8
  extended-cab models, 7 ill.
  sport utility vehicles vs., 4–6
Polytarps, 126
Programmable Read Only Memory
  chips (PROMs), 155–56

Racing
  transmissions for, 71
  wheels for, 48
Radial tires, 41
Radiator(s), 151, *see also* Antifreeze;
  Coolant
  inspection, 21
Rated line pull (RLP), 97–99
Rocks, 118, 119
Roof racks, 145, 167–68
Running boards, 140
Rust, 19, 159, 168
Ruts, 114–15

Safety chains, 108–109
Salt, road, 112
Scratches, 159–60

Search-and-rescue operations, 117
Servicing, *see also* Maintenance
  schedules
Shock absorbers, 19, 28, 30, 32–33,
  34, 36–37
Sidewall tires, 41
Skidding, 45
Sleeping bags, 122–23
Sleeve type, of leaf-spring applications, 33
Slippage, 70–71, 150
Snatch blocks, 100–101
Society of Automotive Engineers
  (SAE), 133
Spark plugs
  boots and wires, 151
  inspecting, 21
Speed
  momentum vs., 114
  in offroad driving, 44–45, 63,
    113–14
Speedometer reading
  new wheels and tires and, 58
Sporting vehicles, *see also* Pickups;
  Sport utility vehicles
  compact vs. full-size, 4–6
  "computer," 154–58
  for deer hunters, 137–42
  equipment, 6–10
  for fishing, 142–47
  immobilization of, 166
  interiors, 6–7, 19
  markets for, 153–54, 155
  new
    choosing, 4–6
    cost, 4, 6, 10–12
    leasing, 13
    purchasing, 3–14
    researching, 10–11
    types, 3–4
  purposes of, 32, 33, 153–54
  security of, 165–67
  "soft," 31–32, 154
  soft cap for, 143–44

suburbanization of, 153–54
used
  checklist, 173–75
  cost, 15, 23–24, 154
  examination of, 18–23
  profile of, 16–17
  purchasing, 15–26
  test driving, 22–23
  wear and tear, 17–18
  washing of, 168–69
Sport utility vehicles
  pickups vs., 4–6
Springs, 19, *see also* Suspension
  air, 33–34
Starter(s)
  insulating, 151
Steering
  inspecting, 22
Steering wheel
  suspension and, 27–29
Storage, 139–40, 145–47
Stoves, 124–25
Survival tips, 117
Suspension, 18
  inspecting, 22, 27–31
  lift, 34–36
  logbooks and, 30–31
  softening of, 31–34, 154
  towing and, 31
  upgrading, 32–34

Tables, camp, 125–26
Tailgate, 19
Tailpipe
  inspecting, 20
Temperature gauges, 150, 164
  engine oil, 164
  transmission fluid, 72, 75, 164
Tents, 121–22
Test driving, 22–23
Thefts, 165–67
Tires
  brake upgrades and, 81
  cost, 41

highway all-season, 39
highway rib, 38–39
inflation pressure, 42–43
light-truck, 41
load-carrying capacity, 42
maximum-traction offroad, 40
offroad/all-terrain, 39
radial, 41
replacement of, 30, 41
shock absorbers and, 37
shoulder areas, 40
sidewalls, 41
size
  gears and, 53, 57–60, 66
  performance and, 56
  wheels and, 51–52
traction and, 39–40
tread design, 39, 40
upgrading, 151
wear, 19
wheels and, 41–42, 49–50,
  51–52
Tongue weight (TW), 105
Torque
  curve, 56
  gear ratios and, 55
  rating, 7–8
Towing, 32, 76, *see also* Hitches;
  Trailers
  brake rotors and, 81
  heat and, 73–74
  hitches, 104–12
  inspection tips, 111–12
  packages, 9
  suspension and, 31
  vehicle size vs. load size, 73–74
Tracking, 22
Traction
  brakes and, 82–84
  tires and, 39–40
Trade-ins, 25
Trailers, *see also* Hitches; Towing
  backing up, 110–11
  level-riding, 109–10

Trailers *(continued)*
lights, 112
tire pressure, 112
weight ratings, 105
wheel hubs, 112
wiring systems, 107-108
Trails, *see also* Offroad driving
changes in, 116-17, 118
obstacles, 118-19,
see also Ruts
Transmission(s)
accessories, 71-72
automatic transmission fluid
(ATF), *see* Automatic transmission fluid (ATF)
automatic vs. manual, 8, 145
auxiliary coolers, 138, 150
auxiliary oil coolers, 69, 71, 74,
150
cooling of, 68-69
draining oil from, 74
heat and, 69, 74, 150
inspecting, 22
maintenance of, 69-70
modification for deer hunting,
138-39
oil pans, 71
remote filters, 72
slippage, 70-71
temperature gauges, 72, 75
Trucks, *see* Pickups; Sporting
vehicles
Two-wheel drive vehicles
full-locking differentials in,
63-64

Used car lots, 25

Vacuum gauges, 165
Valve body recalibration kits, 70, 72,
150
Valving, shock absorbers and, 37
Viscosity, 133-35
Volatility, 135

Warranty, effect of upgrades on,
156-57
Weather conditions, 117, 133-34
Weight
rating of, 104-105
RLP and, 97
in towing, 73-74
transfer, 84
Wheels
aluminum, 46-49
billet, 47
bolt circles, 50
brake upgrades and, 81
cast, 47
fit, 49-52
forged, 47-49
installation, 51-52
load rating and, 50
locks for, 166-67
offset, 50-51
racing and, 48
replacement, 30
rim size, 41-42
size, 49-50
spinning, 69, 70 ill., 114
steel, 46, 48
tires and, 41-42, 51-52
vehicle handling and, 48
Wheel wells
washing, 169
Winches, 96-103, 141, 145, 152,
162-63
accessories, 99
anchor points for, 100-101
cable length, 98-99
double-line pull, 100-101
gears, 99
motors, 99
operation, 100-101, 102-103
RLP of, 97-99
selection, 97-99
single-line pull, 100
Windows, 19
Windshield wipers, 112